WE ARE
STILL HERE

An anthology of resilience, grief, and unshattered
hope from Gaza's university students

Edited by
Zahid Pranjol & Jacob Norris

Daraja Press

Published by
Daraja Press
https://darajapress.com
Wakefield, Quebec, Canada
2025

ISBN: 9781997742043 (soft cover)
ISBN: 9781997742050 (ePub)

Cover design and typesetting: Kate McDonnell

Library and Archives Canada Cataloguing in Publication

Title: We are still here : an anthology of resilience, grief, and unshattered hope from Gaza's
    university students / editors, Zahid Prajol and Jacob Norris.
Other titles: We are still here (2025)
Names: Pranjol, Zahid, editor. | Norris, Jacob, editor.
Identifiers: Canadiana (print) 20250259400 | Canadiana (ebook) 2025026384X |
    ISBN 9781997742043 (softcover) | IS3N 9781997742050 (EPUB)
Subjects: LCSH: Israel-Hamas War, 2023-—Poetry. | LCSH: Gaza Strip—History—
    Bombardment, 2023-— Poetry. | LCSH: English poetry—Gaza Strip. | LCSH: College
    students' writings. | LCGFT: War poetry. | LCGFT: Poetry.
Classification: LCC PR9570.P342 W42 2025 | DDC 821/.9208035856943055—dc23

The one who offers the eulogy
is the most miserable of all.

– Mariam Marwan Malaka

To all the Palestinian students—
the displaced, the starved, the grieving, the silenced.
To those whose dreams were shattered mid-sentence,
whose classrooms turned to rubble,
whose futures were buried before they could begin.
This book is for you.
To carry your voices beyond the checkpoints,
across borders, and into the hearts of the world.

Table of contents

POEMS

Prologue

Since April 2024, we have been working closely with students from Gaza's universities, trying to offer support as Israel systematically destroyed Gaza's academic infrastructure. We began by providing teaching materials, research mentorship and English language training. Quickly we realised the students possess an indomitable urge to write and to bear witness. As we listened to their words, we were deeply moved by their beauty and power, ever more convinced of the need to disseminate them to the outside world. Here, we present a selection of their creative works – pieces that capture their pain, hopes, and reflections.

Many of these short essays and poems were jotted down on scraps of paper amidst the rubble, their authors unsure if they would be alive the next day. Some were written originally in English, others in Arabic. All have made their way into this book through a collaborative process of translation and editing in which the students themselves have taken the lead. The aim throughout has been to preserve the sense of urgency and raw emotion in which the pieces were forged.

The students are not celebrated writers or published authors. They are ordinary young people living through a genocide, trying to make sense of the unfathomable. Each contribution is a living testimony to the strength of a generation that continues to persevere, resist, and express – even in the darkest of times.

The deliberate targeting and killing of academics and students means that some of the young voices who contributed to this book may no longer be alive by the time you read these words. Nevertheless, their spirits continue to proclaim: *We Are Still Here*.

We hope their words touch your hearts and leave a lasting impression.

Zahid Pranjol and Jacob Norris (editors), University of Sussex

▲ Al-Azhar University before

Al-Azhar University after ▼

We Are Still Here:
Voices from Gaza's Student Generation

This book is not simply a collection of stories and poems.

It is a heartbeat.

A cry.

A testament.

We had visions of graduation ceremonies, of family celebrations, of waking up to ordinary mornings. Instead, we woke up to war. Starvation. Silence.

We live under siege, stripped not only of food and shelter, but of the most basic elements of humanity, agency, and safety. In a world that has turned its face away, where our stories are lost beneath the rubble and the headlines, we write – because writing is resistance.

We write while hungry.

We write by candlelight, under the hum of drones.

We write without knowing whether we will survive the night.

This book gives us something the world has denied us: a voice.

Here, you will find fragments of lives interrupted, hopes deferred, and futures on pause. But you will also find resilience. In every verse and every memory, we defy erasure. We document our pain, our yearning, our strength and, above all, our unwavering humanity.

Read these words not as distant tragedies, but as real-time truths. Listen to them. Carry them. Let them echo.

Because to be heard is to exist.

And we refuse to disappear in silence.

Written by university students of Gaza, Palestine

REFLECTIONS

Those I loved have departed

Dunia Raafat Shamia

A great light spreads across the city, and across my heart too.
    I no longer have time to mourn the way I used to, nor to offer
    myself even a moment of peace.
The days pass without change, and all I feel is despair. I stumble
    around my room, hoping to come to my senses – but I don't.
An endless internal struggle without rest. Voices in my head strong
    enough to bring me to my knees.
How do you save yourself when you're all alone?
How do you rescue yourself from... yourself?
Life has always been hard – full of trials and confusion – but these
    days are the cruelest of all.

I am Dunia, daughter of the martyr Raafat. I haven't yet turned twenty.
I lost my father in the 2008 war. I never healed from the pain of that
    loss. I grew up fatherless.
My uncle loved me dearly, and I loved him even more. He was my
    pillar, the one who reminded me most of my father – may God
    have mercy on him.
We used to drink coffee together. I'd light up when he visited, and
    I'd scold him when he didn't.
But on October 7, 2023, fate took him too. My hero left me, and life
    hasn't been the same.
When I heard he was martyred, my legs gave out. A loud buzzing, then
    silence. I collapsed, powerless.
I screamed, "Liars! Liars!" – I didn't know if the words came from my
    mouth or my shattered heart.
Tears scorched my cheeks. I just wanted to wake from this nightmare
    and find him alive.

Then, on another wretched day, I was reading a book to comfort myself
    when my brother burst in:
"They bombed Auntie's house – she might be martyred."
He left to check. Hours crawled by like eternity until he returned,
    carrying her child:
"She's gone. Her husband's in critical condition – pray he survives so
    the boy's not left alone."

And oh – how the heart burns before the tears even fall.
I hadn't healed from my uncle's death, and now my aunt, my dearest
    friend and sister in one, was gone.
She knew every detail of my life. Nidaa is gone. My beloved has
    departed, and I am alone.
She won't stay up with me anymore. I won't see her radiant smile or
    hear her say I'm her soul's joy.
Nidaa is gone – to join my father and my uncle.

Days later, while we were trapped in her house under siege,
    all communication was cut.
No phones, no messages. Just the sounds of shelling and gunfire.
We sat in silence, unsure if we would live to see another day.
When the army pulled back, and we were left to face what remained
    of our grief, my cousin called my mother:
"Her brother has been martyred."
My gentle uncle, Abu Riyad, killed by a treacherous missile.
I felt nothing. Just emptiness.
Will all my loved ones leave me?
How easy it is – for the innocent to be burned, shattered, erased –
    at the click of a button.
I once loved technology and progress. Now I loathe them – and those
    who made them.

Abu Riyad has gone to join my aunt and uncle.
They all left me – alone.
They left behind a trembling heart.

I am Dunia. Daughter of Gaza the Proud.
Daughter of a people of dignity, generosity, and honour.
Never did I imagine I would starve. I was always among those
    who gave.
Now I stand among half a million others in Northern Gaza with
    empty hands and aching stomachs.
We refused to flee our homes or surrender to the occupier –
    and so they punished us.
No food, no water.
Is this how they hope to force us into submission?
By starving our children, tormenting our women,
    slaughtering our youth before their mothers' eyes?

But it wasn't enough for them to separate us from our martyrs.
They tore the living apart too.
How could I forget how they split me from my brother –
    my joy, my laughter, my other half?
He was trapped in the south, and I in the north, prevented from
    reuniting by their checkpoints.
How could I forget the distance from my grandfather's house –
    destroyed by bombs – forcing them to flee south?

Curse them. Did they forget that this land is ours?

When Bombs Wake You Instead of the Alarm

Sara Aaed Abass Alkhaldy

It was the weekend – Thursday. I came back from university and stepped into my beloved home. I kissed my mother and carried on with my day as I pleased.

My professor – who is now a martyr – had told us that there would be a short exam the following Tuesday, and that we should study well. I studied on Friday, then set my alarm for Saturday morning so I could continue. But before the alarm could wake me, I was jolted awake by the sound of missiles. Yes, it was October 7th – our second Nakba.

We were displaced from our home without our cherished belongings, without even enough clothes. I remember that feeling vividly. I wished I could carry the entire house with me – with all its corners, and all its memories, both sad and joyful – in my university backpack that I fled with. I wished I could bottle the scent of our home and take it with me as I left. But it was no use.

A few days later, we learned that our house had been destroyed, everything inside reduced to rubble. I swear I heard my heart break at that very moment.

We were displaced from one place to another. In the summer, we stayed in a tent. It was like a blazing oven, a place not even an animal could endure.

On another day, we ran, carrying nothing but our lives, fleeing the bullets of the occupation. We ended up sitting in the street. I remember looking up at the sky for a long time. I think that's when I truly grew up. I understood what it means to have a home, what it means to be displaced, what it means to sleep on the street with nothing but your soul.

Then we were displaced again, and again – until this very moment, where we are deprived even of food. There is nothing to eat. We sleep and wake to the ache of hunger, but we thank God we are still alive.

Yet the tragedy continues. And no one knows how – or when – it will end.

Silence of shards

Hada Mohammed Homaid

One day, a hopeful, ambitious girl stood at the edge of a new beginning, ready to take her first step toward a carefully planned future. But, as we all know, the winds do not always favor a ship's course.

Without warning, Hada's life was overtaken by relentless nightmares that shattered her well-ordered world.

Exactly 645 days ago, she was 18 – driven, passionate, and full of promise. She lived with her mother, father, and youngest brother. Her extended family – two married sisters, brothers, nieces, and nephews – were deeply bound by love and shared dreams.

She had just graduated from high school with a remarkable GPA of 99.4. Her heart was set on studying English Literature, a major she chose with joy. But before the journey could begin, war broke out.

In the chaos, her family was torn apart. Forced from their home, they sought shelter in the south of Gaza. Days blurred into nights – some carrying small joys, most marked by hunger, fear, and uncertainty.

There was no news of her father. Was he alive? Was he starving like so many others? After days of silence and unbearable waiting, a breakthrough came: a negotiated return home.

But what waited for them was not home – it was rubble. Their three apartments and family house were destroyed. Still, they were grateful. None of them were physically harmed, and in a land of grief, survival was a blessing.

They tried to rebuild what they could of their lives, moving into a rented house. Hope flickered. Maybe, somehow, stability could return.

Then, as history tragically repeats itself, the ceasefire was shattered. A surprise attack struck during what was supposed to be a time of peace. The siege grew tighter. Food, medicine – even basic necessities – were cut off.

They endured.

Until June 4, 2025.

On that day, the sun did not rise for Hada and her family. Her eldest brother – her guide, her second parent, her heart's anchor – was killed in a direct attack.

He was more than a brother. He was a father of five young children, a devoted husband, a cherished son, a noble soul. His name was **Al-Hassan**, meaning *the virtuous* – a name he lived up to in every way. Honest. Gentle. Brave.

His death tore a hole through their world.

He left behind five children without a father, parents without their joy, a wife without her partner, and siblings without their pillar.

Since that day, Hada and her family have struggled to rise. Grief has made the ground beneath them unsteady.

Yet they keep moving.

They carry Al-Hassan's spirit in the lives of his children, in the memories they whisper to each other, and in their prayers – hoping to see him again in dreams, and one day, by God's mercy, on the Day of Judgment.

Life Under the Occupation

Alaa Eyad Saleh Khudier

To this day, the sun of the next morning has not risen.

I am a student at Al-Azhar University in Gaza. Like many others, I once walked into university full of passion, determined to pursue my dream. But because of the Israeli occupation, our lives were disrupted. Our dreams were paused, our classrooms closed. Still, we did not give up.

We held on to our goals. We adapted. We continued our studies online.

I was overjoyed to begin studying the major I had chosen – Translation. I believed that with hard work and dedication, I could become a great translator.

Since school, English had always been my favorite subject. To develop my skills, I completed twelve levels of training at Al-Salam Training Group. That helped, but I knew it wasn't enough. So I chose Al-Azhar University to turn my passion into a profession. I dreamed not only of becoming a skilled translator, but of speaking English fluently.

Every morning, I went to university with energy and enthusiasm.

Then came the morning of Saturday, October 7. At 6:30 a.m., as the birds were just beginning to sing, we heard rockets launched from Gaza. Moments later, the war began – a war of extermination.

No student could return to school or university after that. We were left only with questions: *What just happened? What comes next?*

The occupation began bombing homes, hospitals, and schools. Thousands of civilians – many of them children – were killed. Families were displaced and told to flee to so-called "safe zones." Hospitals were destroyed. The wounded were denied treatment. The occupation even targeted education, destroying schools and universities to silence our minds and voices. They fear an educated people – people like Wafaa Al-Adini and others who dared to speak the truth.

But Palestinians do not surrender.

Even amid blackouts, food shortages, water scarcity, and weak internet, students resumed their studies online.

For me, it was painful not to study on campus, not to sit with my classmates, ask questions, and engage face-to-face. The war destroyed the only space where learning felt possible. I had to switch to online learning.

I couldn't study my first semester – there was no internet where I lived. When it was finally restored, I postponed that semester and enrolled in the second one. I studied, attended every online lecture, revised hard and earned high grades. I registered for another semester, and again I succeeded.

Now I'm in my second year, second semester. And the war still hasn't stopped.

But I am still here. We are still here.

In the end, never give up on your dreams, no matter how difficult the road. Hold on, and you will arrive.

I hope this war ends soon. I hope we rebuild Gaza. And I hope we return to our classrooms – not through screens, but side by side – ready to learn, grow, and live the futures we've been fighting for.

Our Second Displacement – in the Sabra Area

Nour Mohammed Abusultan

In our second displacement, we had taken shelter in my aunt's home in the Sabra neighborhood. After a month there, the sound of daily bombardment had become almost routine. We thought we were growing used to it – until the nights turned heavier, the bombings more violent.

Each evening after the call to the 'Isha prayer, just as the imam's voice rose with "Allahu Akbar," came the whir of fire belts, the shelling, the strikes.

I remember one morning we received a call from a private number: the "Israeli Defense Forces" demanding we leave the building. Over 100 people lived in our apartment block. People argued, but we had nowhere else to go. No safe place left.

That day passed until it was time for 'Isha prayer. During the second rak'ah, as the imam said, *"Sami' Allahu liman hamidah,"* the house turned red. Flames engulfed the neighboring building. The pressure shook our own. Glass shattered. Children screamed and wept.

Still, we finished our prayer. Each of us awaited sujood – our moment to plead with God. My lips whispered: *"Hasbunallahu wa ni'mal wakeel... O Allah, our hearts are at our throats!"*

Afterward, we gathered as usual around the radio: "Any news? Give us hope." A ceasefire was being negotiated. The skies above Lod glowed dimly. We waited for illumination bombs to light the night.

We talked. Each person gave their analysis. Like always – until sleep called.

2:30 AM

Relentless shelling. We huddled close. Mothers clutched their children. Our tongues echoed the shahada: *"I bear witness there is no god but Allah, and Muhammad is His messenger."*

We tried to sleep – but the bombing only intensified. Bullets, artillery, drones, flares, gas bombs. The call to Fajr prayer sounded. We rushed to pray.

"If we're fated to die, let it be in prayer," someone said.

"I'd rather die praying," said another.

"Pray for them, curse them while you pray."

We read the morning supplications. I don't know how I slept – maybe an hour.

Then came the command:

"Girls, get downstairs – everyone, go!"

We searched for our mothers, sisters, fathers.

The women gathered in one apartment, the men in another across the way.

8:00 AM

The street between us and the neighboring building was littered with leaflets – dropped from above:

"Evacuate to the south. This is your final warning."

We rushed to pack. IDs, papers, a change of clothes – anything we could grab. Some wanted to flee. Others insisted on staying.

I, in tears, went to make wudu and pray istikhara.

Just as I finished my final salaam, a missile struck the roof.
It felt like a sign from God: It's time to go.
"O Allah, we place our trust in You. Choose for us, not against us."

We gathered at the building entrance – over 100 of us.
We raised white flags. We whispered the shahada. Tears welled
     in every eye.
Then came news: those who tried to leave from the neighboring
     building were struck by a tank shell – some injured.
Panic. Our hearts beat like war drums.
If we stayed, the house would collapse. If we left, we might be
     bombed in the street.

The men came:
"Trust in God. Walk in line. Hold the white flags. Follow Ahmad."
Each of us strapped a bag to our backs, raised a flag in one hand,
     and our index finger in the other.
"I bear witness that there is no god but Allah, and Muhammad is
     His messenger."

I tried to hold back my tears and steady my steps.
I don't know how I walked, but I walked.
I scanned the crowd for my parents and sisters – then I saw my father
     carrying my little sister on his shoulders, repeating the *shahada*.
He looked lost – my father, who had always been my strength, now
     unsure of where to go, what to do.

We walked until we reached Asqoula roundabout.
     There, the crowd scattered.
The news was cut off.
We now faced a choice: head south – or find shelter with relatives in
     the Zeitoun neighborhood.

Resilient Rula, A reflection from Gaza

Rula Ibrahim Abu ElKhair

I am Rula Ibrahim Abu Al-Khair, 20 years old, a second-year medical student living in Gaza City.

This is not just my story – this is my soul speaking through rubble, fear, and a relentless will to keep going. When the war broke out, I had just started living my dream. I had entered medicine college at one of the best universities Al Azhar university of Gaza – something I had worked for with passion and dedication. I only attended one week of classes before everything shattered. One night, heavy bombing shook our neighborhood, and we were ordered to evacuate. I was shocked, confused, and scared. We fled to Khan Younis, carrying only essentials. I didn't even take the gold necklace my parents gifted me ten years ago which means a lot to me.The fear controlled me after that tragic night, I just grabbed a few clothes and my iPad.

That was the beginning of five displacements. Each one was harder than the other. From Gaza to Khan Younis, then to Rafah, and back again. I tried to travel to Egypt and continue my study at Cairo University, but the Israeli army attacked Rafah and closed the crossing. I lost that chance.

I lost a whole academic year.

But I didn't lose my hope...

When my university decided to resume online classes, which was a crazy idea while the war was still flaring up, my mum encouraged me to continue my education online despite the situation and to struggle for my future, so I made a decision: whatever the matter was, I would always remember the quotation:

When it feels scary to jump that's exactly when you jump, otherwise you end up staying in the same place your whole life.

Even in places with no electricity, no water, and no stable internet, I installed an eSIM on my phone and climbed to the rooftop under buzzing drones to download lectures. I took exams in cafés by the sea. I studied while hungry, while afraid, while grieving.

I decided to live as a survivor not as a victim.

This is my reflection-not only on survival, but on persistence. On the battle between despair and purpose. I lost friends medical colleagues, and all sense of normalcy. I watched as some of Gaza's greatest doctors were martyred while saving lives. But that gave me more reason to continue.

I want to be part of rebuilding the medical field. I want to serve my people-not just as a doctor, but as a source of healing. I believe medicine is more than treating diseases. It's about serving humanity, especially in places like Gaza, where war never stops, neither do we.

I want the world to know: we are not just headlines. We are hearts, dreams, and futures. I want to be a hero-first for myself, then for my family, and for every patient I will help one day.

Being steadfast is more than just a word It's waking up and studying with drones above. It's continuing to dream when everything around you is falling apart. And maybe, just maybe, that's what makes us unstoppable.

I am Rula and I am resilient ...

Believe that life is not about waiting for the storm to pass...it is about to dance in the rain. No matter what the circumstances may be, the ability to continue is a decision in your mind

---

Hope from Beneath the Rubble

Alaa Maher Al.Zebda

One moment, we were stepping into medical school with dreams
    in our eyes – and the next, we were sinking into a dark swamp,
    with no light in sight.
But from within that darkness, a faint glow emerged: the flicker of
    hope inside us.
We are living through the worst moments anyone could endure –
    moments we wouldn't wish on anyone.

Imagine spending years building a future, working tirelessly,
    striving to make your family proud – only to find yourself
    back at zero, with nothing.
Everything you built – gone.

Everyone who supported you – disappeared.
Your home destroyed, leaving you in the streets.
Your friends killed – you're left without a companion.
Your pet buried beneath the rubble.
Your university turned to ruins.
Your white coat, your dream of medicine, burned before your eyes.
You've lost everything – material and emotional – and you're left
    stunned, asking: *What now?*

And yet… despite it all, you carry the certainty that you're still strong.
That this too shall pass.
That your will can create a miracle.

We made a vow: just as we fought through every obstacle to become
    doctors, we will bring hope to the lives of those who suffer.
We see death in front of us every second.
We sleep hungry – in bitter cold or scorching heat.
We have no medicine when we fall ill, and everything around us
    seems to attack us.

Still, we believe our willpower will prevail.
We let the passion within us break free.
From the ashes of our shattered dreams, a fierce light emerges.
We begin again – drawing a new future in black and white.

Imagine starting from nothing – after you were so close to everything.
I often marvel at our strength: how did we keep going in a place
    where every step forward drags you ten steps back?

Our choices are few, and all of them hard.
But even bitter choices are better than standing still, defeated.
With faith in ourselves, we created new goals and new dreams.
We paved new paths – and now, we walk them, despite it all.

We continued our studies, even if not within university walls.
We try to adapt to life in tents, even without the most basic necessities.
We've endured every forced displacement, every exile from our land.
We've forgotten what stability means – but we believe these days
    will end, and we'll redraw our lives with colored pens.

We try to sleep after exhausting days – closing our eyes to the sound of
explosions, our hearts anxious for what morning might bring.
We study each other's faces carefully, just in case we're separated forever.

We know if death comes, we won't escape it.
But we're determined to keep going.

It may sound trivial, but imagine waking up with work or classes ahead
– and you can't even start the day with coffee.
Even that was taken from us.
We study and work on empty stomachs, under the roar of warplanes
and cries of wounded children.
We walk long distances just to find a signal to study online.

Truly, it must be God giving us the strength to endure all this –
without Him, we would've lost hope long ago.

Yes, we go through moments of depression and pressure –
but we rise again.
Because if you don't, it will consume you.

In this life, survival belongs to the strongest – not in muscle, but in faith.
Faith that this too will change.

Just as we live these painful days, we will one day live peaceful,
beautiful ones.
Days where we rebuild our lives...

Even if not in this world – then in Paradise, which is worth more
than a million fading worlds.

The 7th of October

Shahd Mahmoud Almadhoun

As always, since my very first day at university – as a first-year
engineering student at the Islamic University – I would get ready
early to reach campus before lectures began, so I could share
breakfast with my cousin Basmala in our usual spot.

My mother would be waking my siblings so they wouldn't miss
    the car to school. It was an ordinary, perfectly routine morning –
Until everything stopped.

A sound shook every corner of our city.
At first, with winter approaching, we didn't know if it was thunder…
    or something our enemy feared more than thunder.
The noise grew louder and went on for nearly half an hour –
Then we found out: it was the resistance launching rockets.

That morning, my cousin Amal had messaged me – we had planned
    the night before to go to university together:
Shahd, your class is at 8, right? But let's head out early – like 7:15?"
I joked back: *"Looks like we're not going anywhere."*
I didn't know then… that it would be my last day of university until
    who knows when.

Today is day 113 since October 7.
Once again, we wait – unsure if a "humanitarian truce" will be
    announced or broken before it begins.
It's the 113th day of a war we knew was inescapable – a war we
    entered only after we truly shook them.
And now, we face destruction, genocide, brutality, arrogance.
Our bodies are exhausted, our faces hollow, our spirits dimmed.

But one thing hasn't changed:
Our love for this land, our unwavering support for the resistance.
We've grown even more rooted – more in love with Gaza,
this Gaza we cannot bear to be separated from,
this Gaza now scarred and ruined, as though time has dragged it fifty
    years into the past.

This war is unlike any before.
More than three months in, still raging.
I never imagined it would last this long – or that we would last
    this long.
God help us.

I don't even know how many days have passed since
    the genocide began.
I only know it's been more than a year.
But I've stopped counting.

More than that – I've stopped feeling like myself.
I haven't adapted. But I try.
I try to become the version of myself I once dreamed of.

There's still a flicker of hope in my soul.
It tells me I will return to myself –
Proud of who I've become.
I don't know when…
But I will. Without a doubt.

Into the Abyss: How War Pulled Our Humanity Down

Saad Aldin Ahmed Muhanna

The day an old woman kicked an empty water bottle and cursed at
   a child trying to beat her to the queue – I knew we had reached
   rock bottom.

We're no longer who we used to be.
Not me.
Not the people.
Not anything.

Since the war began, and with every wave of displacement, we've been
   uprooted from one place and thrown into another – a school one
   day, a mosque the next, then a tattered tent barely big enough for
   the ghost of a human being.

Eventually, even space itself couldn't hold us – not even for a breath.

People piled up – not like bodies, but like layers of class, dignity,
   and morality crammed into a pot with no lid.
They melted.
Evaporated.
And from them rose a new layer… nameless, but lower than anything
   that came before it.

There was once a time when people said:
"He's respectable."
"She's educated."

"She comes from such-and-such family."
All of that shattered the moment someone tossed down
  a bottle of water from a truck, and the crowd lunged for it
  like starving wolves.

Here, you cannot afford decency.
If you wait your turn – you lose it.
If you show respect – you get robbed.
If you try to remain "a decent human being" – you get trampled.

With time, I learned to shout.
To shove.
To speak in a tone that isn't mine, with a voice I never thought I had.
I became one of them.
Or maybe I always was – and only ever lived under conditions that let
  me pretend to be rational.

We are not just fighting to survive.
We're fighting not to lose ourselves completely while trying to survive.

Each night, I return to my corner of the tent.
I look at the faces around me.
Then I reach into my chest to feel –
Is there still something alive inside me?

Sometimes, I find it.
Sometimes, I don't.

And I ask myself:
Will this war ever end?
And if it does – will I remember how to be human again?
Or will I carry this wilderness within me… forever?

Screams Echoing

Farah Talal Mohammed Abomutayer

The screams echoed from the operating room –
a wounded man crying out as surgeons performed amputations
  and extracted shrapnel.
There was no anesthesia.
No sterile tools.

Just basic instruments on a cold, bloodied floor, overwhelmed by
the chaos of crowds, casualties, and desperation.

That scream belonged to Osama.

He had already lost a limb in a previous strike, and now another
surgery was underway – shrapnel had torn through his stomach,
damaging vital organs.
Six long hours passed.
No modern equipment. No painkillers. No antibiotics – because the
blockade has choked Gaza's hospitals, cutting off medicine and
supplies.

Still, miraculously, the surgery succeeded.

Osama later recounted the story of his injury.
It happened in Jabalia Camp.
A drone launched a missile at a group of civilians – unarmed people
simply checking on one another.
The strike left a trail of martyrs and the wounded.
Osama survived – but not whole.
That strike shattered not only bodies, but lives – taking limbs, futures,
and the warmth of friendships that would never return.

An ambulance fought its way through rubble and obstacles to reach
the site.
The road was harsh – strewn with stones, debris, and the ruins of homes.
In Gaza, there's no safety – not for civilians, not for medics, not even
for the dead.
The ambulance crew whispered prayers the whole way, begging to
reach the hospital before another missile fell.

Osama had already lost his mother in November.
His sister and wife followed in December.
Now, in January, he survived – again.
But he had seen it all: fear, hunger, cold, grief etched into the eyes
of his younger siblings.

When he was discharged, Osama returned to what remained
of his neighborhood.

He went looking for his friends.
He went to the cemetery – he had learned that four of them were gone.
They had seen the worst of this world before they left it:

the racism, the lies, the hypocrisy…
a world where children in Gaza are sentenced to die – hungry, cold,
and bleeding – while children elsewhere are held in warmth, safety,
and peace.

He recited *Al-Fatiha* over their graves.
Memories fell like rain –
laughter, sorrow, shared moments, lost time.

Overhead, the hated roar of jets grew louder.
It was a familiar sign.
Something was coming.

And then – it happened.
Multiple strikes.
A belt of fire lit up the skies.
Another massacre.
More martyrs.

Among them was Osama.

He joined his loved ones –
his wife, his mother, his sister.
The woman he loved, the one he wept for – now reunited with him
in a better place.

He died with a smile on his face.
As if, finally, he had found what he had always longed for:
Reunion.
Safety.
Peace.

The kind this world never gave him.

Gaza Is Dying... A Testimony from the Heart of the Health System Collapse

Mohaned Jehad Youssef Alnajjar

In the heart of Gaza, where I volunteered in the health sector, I witnessed an unprecedented collapse of the medical system under the weight of Israel's relentless assault since October 2023.

North and South Without Medical Services

In the north, hospitals like the Indonesian Hospital, Kamal Adwan, and Al-Awda were forced out of service after the Israeli army declared them active combat zones. In Rafah, following widespread destruction, medical teams ceased work entirely. As a result, both northern Gaza and Rafah were left with no functioning medical services.

Hospitals Under Attack

In Gaza City, Al-Shifa Medical Complex – the beating heart of the health system – was bombed and completely destroyed. Several medical staff and patients were killed; others were detained, including Dr. Adnan Al-Bursh, who later died in Israeli custody. The Baptist Hospital (Al-Ma'madani) was also partially destroyed and now stands on the verge of closure.

The Situation in Khan Younis

In Khan Younis, the European Hospital was shut down following a ground invasion. Only Al-Aqsa Martyrs Hospital remains operational in the south, putting immense pressure on already overstretched medical teams and facilities.

A Severe Shortage of Resources

After the Health Ministry announced the reopening of a damaged wing at Al-Shifa, I volunteered to assist. I saw firsthand the critical shortage of doctors and nurses, many of whom were targeted or killed. Operating rooms were few, medical supplies scarce and often unsterilized – raising the risk of infection with every procedure.

Grave and Complex Injuries

The injuries we received were horrifying – deep burns and disfigurements caused by incendiary weapons. These cases require intensive, specialized care that we simply cannot provide under current conditions.

A Plea to End the War

This situation is beyond unbearable. The healthcare system is
    collapsing. Medical teams are working under extreme pressure.
atients are suffering without adequate care.
It is time to end this war.
We need immediate access for humanitarian and medical aid
    to save what lives we still can.

I am just a volunteer in Gaza's hospitals – not yet a doctor –
    but I see the disaster with my own eyes.
The health sector is crumbling.
Hospitals lie in ruins.
Staff are exhausted.
Supplies are nearly gone.

The wounded are many. The pain is overwhelming.
This is not just a health crisis –
It is the collapse of humanity itself.

We Came Back from the Dead

Mohaned Jehad Youssef Alnajjar

On the 23rd of December, the morning arrived cloaked in fear.
Israeli forces advanced on our small town, trailing the stench of
    death and gunpowder, under a barrage of fire unlike anything
    we'd seen before.
The roar of aircraft never ceased. Bullets screamed through the skies.
    Buildings collapsed like autumn leaves.
Children's cries mingled with mothers' prayers, and worry etched itself
    onto faces that had known nothing but hardship.

In the midst of it all, we were there – fleeing not just with our feet,
    but with our prayers, clinging desperately to life.
We were displaced.
We left everything behind: our home, our memories,
    the photos on the walls – even the children's toys.

We survived by a miracle, as if God had pulled us from death's grip
    at the final moment.

Since that day, the night has become terrifying.
No true sleep – only waiting for the next explosion.
We measure safety by the sound of planes.
When they're gone, we exhale – briefly.
When they return, we pull the blankets over our heads and brace
    for what comes next.

And still – we write.
We write to say we were here.
That we resisted death not only with defiance,
but with our stories,
our resilience,
and our refusal to stop living.

Everything burned... except my determination

Wissam Yousef

My name is Wissam Yousef. I was born and raised in Rafah, Gaza, in
a modest family of nine. Since childhood, I excelled in school, earning
top grades and taking part in many activities. I even travelled to Dubai
during middle school to represent the children of Gaza at a conference.

I studied Civil Engineering at the Islamic University. In my final
year, I got married and moved to Egypt, hoping to return and finish
my degree. But after the revolution, political conditions made travel
to and from Gaza nearly impossible. For years, I couldn't see my
family. When I finally had the chance, financial obstacles kept me from
returning. I couldn't afford the trip – or the tuition.

Then came another blow: my husband lost his legal residency in Egypt.
We couldn't enroll our children in school without residency permits.
We had to abandon our home, his job, and the life we had built. We
returned to Gaza in 2022 – our first displacement. We came back to
nothing. No home, no income, no furniture.

We lived with my family until my husband – an architect – found work. Slowly, life began to mend. The children went back to school. We built a small room and a bathroom above my parents' apartment. It was simple, but safe. I promised myself I would never leave my country again.

But on October 7, everything changed. Gaza was no longer safe.
My husband lost his job.
Our children had to leave school.
Then came our second displacement, forced out of my parents' home in Rafah under fire – leaving everything behind again, not even clothes, food, or essentials.

We ended up in a relative's house in Khan Younis. We had nothing. I was pregnant with my fourth child. No medical care, no nutrition, no prenatal vitamins. I was terrified of giving birth during war – especially since I needed a C-section.

On July 26, 2024, I gave birth to my daughter –
On a day of intense shelling near eastern Khan Younis.
The hospital was overwhelmed with the wounded.
There were no painkillers, no post-op care.
My surgery was difficult due to internal adhesions, and I lay in agony, unable to breastfeed my newborn. She weighed just 2.5 kg and needed neonatal care due to jaundice.

Still, we were forced to leave the hospital the next day – there were no beds, only emergencies.
We returned to my relatives' home. No transport. No bed.
No nourishment to help my recovery or feed my baby.
This is what war looks like for pregnant and nursing mothers.

Two weeks later, we woke to explosions as nearby buildings were destroyed at random. Screams filled the air. We ran again, in panic. This was our third displacement.

Imagine it – me, my husband, and four children, one of them just two weeks old, and the others sick with chickenpox. We had nothing, not even transport.
We walked until we found a donkey cart that took us to Al-Mawasi, where my aunt gave us a tent beside hers.

Do you know what it's like to live in a tent during Gaza's summer?

Extreme heat. Limited water. Overflowing trash.
Open sewage. Insects. Rodents. Stray dogs trying to enter the tent at
night.
Noise. Chaos. Drones buzzing overhead.
Contagious diseases. Scabies. Meningitis.

My baby turned one month old – and was diagnosed with meningitis,
a disease that spread during the war due to malnutrition and low
immunity.
She was hospitalized for ten days – away from her father and siblings.
The isolation ward was overcrowded. I slept on the floor with her.
No beds, no rest. Meanwhile, my other children suffered alone outside.

Eventually, we returned. But the area was unsafe – again.
And so came our fourth displacement.

This time, to a school-turned-shelter – Qandila School near
Nasser Hospital.
It had been bombed and burned, barely standing.
To get a space inside, you had to fight your way through the crowd.
We found a 20-square-meter space. In it, we lived, cooked, washed,
and did everything.

This wasn't life. It wasn't even survival.
Just existence.

There's no cleanliness. No peace. No safety.
People separated by nothing but thin sheets.
Garbage, sewage, insects, skin and respiratory diseases everywhere.

Still, we weren't spared from death.
More than 20 of my relatives were killed.
All our homes were destroyed – mine, my sisters', my uncles', aunts' –
every last one.
We are all in tents now. No one has a home to return to, even when the
war ends.

Now the school itself is under evacuation orders.
Most people have already left – except us and those with nowhere else
to go, no strength to flee again, no money to move.
We stay. We hide.

Tanks are nearby. Shells are hitting randomly.
We wait – for death, or a ceasefire.

And still, I've decided to finish my degree.
I hope to find work after this war – to help my husband,
to rebuild our life.

Studying in war is its own battle.
I can barely pay the university to sit exams.
Internet is often cut – even during tests.
And being a student in war is hard enough.
Being a married student in war – even harder.

This is the brief version of my story.
I wrote it for two reasons:
First – to finally admit it to myself.
And second – to release it from within me.

Throughout this war, I've had to stay strong.
For my husband, so he wouldn't collapse.
For my children, so they wouldn't lose hope.
For others, so they wouldn't pity me.

But inside –
I carry a pain I never imagined I would live through.
A defeat.
A humiliation.
A sorrow too vast for words.

A compassionate land that grew harsh

Saja Abdel Hakim

In each of our eyes lives a Palestinian cry and an Arab sorrow
     that has weighed heavily on our hearts.
The hair of our children has greyed.
The spark of passion in our eyes has faded.
Our hopes have withered.

Our efforts torn apart.
What we once pursued now seems like a mirage,
    and our homeland lies in ruins.
Even our hearts – those once tender hearts – are no longer
    what they used to be.

This is Gaza.
My beloved homeland.
Here, there is nothing but death.
No sound rises above the sound of weeping.
No feeling outweighs sorrow.
And there is no healing after the shattering pain of loss.

My father – may God have mercy on him – taught me to see this land
    through his eyes.
Through them, I saw it as beautiful, warm, authentic, strong,
    and full of compassion.
He used to say that the dearest place on earth to any soul is their
    homeland – and that **Gaza is the dearest of them all**.

I often told him of my dream to travel abroad after graduating from
    high school,
but I would promise him – *I will return.*
I won't be gone long from the land my father loved, the land where
    he planted his olive trees.
I won't abandon the country where my mother kneads the wheat into
    bread and plants her roses in the soil.
A land where my friends live, where my beloveds and their
    beloveds belong.
I must return.
Just let me leave – for a while – to catch my breath from a siege that
    chokes us,
and I will come back holding a university degree, proud of it –
    and you will be proud of me too.

But my father passed away.
And within a year, I felt the land had changed.
It was no longer as he described.
It had grown cruel.
And all its brothers, cruel with it.
The world holds no heart.
It sees only what it wants to see.

The Flood of al-Aqsa –
That war took my loved ones, and their loved ones and companions.
It placed rubble and dust between us.
So now, the dream of a person living in their homeland is…
       not to remain there.
To leave – and never return.
Forgive me, Father.
Either I escape beyond its borders with no way back…
or I go to Paradise.
And that, truly, is what the heart longs for –
A place where we reunite with our loved ones in an eternal meeting –
a meeting with no more farewells.

A night without dawn

Rasha Ismail Musabeh

We didn't sleep that night.
Terror gripped our hearts and stole our breath.

The occupation's warplanes didn't stop bombing for even a
       single moment.
We were trapped inside this school, unable to leave.

We spent the whole time desperately waiting for morning.
It was the longest night I have ever lived through.
Everything was utterly terrifying.

The glow of the missiles painted the night sky orange,
followed by a sound beyond description –
a sound so powerful I felt my soul might leave my body.
My heart would freeze in those moments, and I'd shut my eyes tight,
convinced they might never open again.

And as soon as morning came,
we rushed to the classroom window to see where the bombs had fallen
       during the night.
But what we saw was shocking –
everything was so close.

I started to tremble.
I begged my family to leave,
but they told me the situation outside was too dangerous.

We have to stay here, they said.
*We have no choice but to die where we are – just like the tens of
    thousands who've already been martyred in this war.*

I couldn't bear those words.
My eyes stayed frozen, fixed on the window, unable to look away
    from the enormous scale of destruction before me.

The whole day I had a feeling –
that something terrible was going to happen to this school.
I didn't know how or when,
but that feeling wouldn't leave me.

At exactly 2:30 in the afternoon,
I was sweeping the classroom, cleaning as usual.
My sister was washing the dishes.
My mother was on the ground floor, buying some bread for lunch.

Then suddenly –
the sound of the nightmare.

A missile hit the center of the schoolyard.
Glass shattered.
Fragments of the rocket rained down on us.

I dropped the broom from my hands
and ran to the door of the classroom, shouting at the top of my voice:
    "Mama! Mama!"

I ran as fast as I could.
All I could see was grey –
the smoke from the missile had blanketed every inch of the school.

When I finally reached the ground floor,
I saw my mother.
I couldn't believe my eyes.

Before I even knew it, I was hugging her tightly,
checking every inch of her – making sure the missile hadn't hurt her.

Then, I shifted my gaze from my mother to the schoolyard –
and saw it soaked in the blood of martyrs.

A chill ran through my body.
I was suddenly reminded of the sacrificial blood we see
    during Eid al-Adha.

But I never imagined **we** would become the sacrifice.

Children lay scattered on the ground.
Elderly men.
Women.

I am talking about a **massacre** –
twenty martyrs whose blood painted the courtyard red.

I couldn't help anyone.
All I could do was **watch** –
silent, wrapped in a shock so deep,
a pain that has not – and will not – be forgotten.

A new day

Lina Khattab

A new day is granted to me. I attempt to live amidst life's hardship, acutely aware of the heroism of humans confronting circumstances they never imagined facing in my small city, the city most insistent on freedom.

Freedom that has become forbidden, where speaking of it is akin to madness. For how can those without a loaf of bread demand a homeland? I have seen with my own eyes how the dreams of the hopeful perish, and what it means to be in a place that allows you nothing beyond the search for food, merely enduring the days.

This reality pains me. And it pains me even more that we are seen merely as human material evoking pity. But here, we are warriors. We battle fear, we dream dreams larger than those we once held, and we live today with the courage to face an end that might be just a bullet or a bomb away as if death holds no terror here, even as we dream of life.

A Survivor's Letter

Malak Al Ashi

*I want to share a message I wrote back in January – believing,
at the time, it might be my last.*

The situation here has been unbearable. Our electricity,
communications, and internet were completely cut off for months.
We were forced to leave our home in Gaza City due to heavy bombing.
But we refused to evacuate to the south of the Strip. Instead, we first
sought shelter at a nearby hospital, and later moved into a residential
building with relatives – still within the same city.

Then the Israeli tanks and soldiers advanced. We were trapped inside
that building, cut off from the world for five long weeks.

There were between 150 and 200 people sheltering inside, 40 of whom
were my own family: my uncles and their children. During that time,
even looking out the window could get you killed – Israeli tanks were
stationed right outside our door. Several apartments in the building
were bombed, including the one we were in. But somehow, by a
miracle, we survived.

They burned and crushed every car in the street, including my father's.
We couldn't go outside to buy food. The municipal water supply had
stopped completely due to the destruction of the infrastructure. We had
only a small amount of drinking water stored. We rationed it carefully,
eating just one meal a day, trying to stretch our supplies in order to stay
alive. At times, we were forced to drink contaminated water that was
unsafe for human consumption.

We saw death, again and again.
We spoke to it.
And every time, it looked us in the eye and said:
"Not yet. I'll come back."

After the tanks and soldiers retreated, we emerged to witness a level of
destruction no human mind could fathom. The entire city was rubble.
The streets we once walked on were unrecognizable – erased by horror.

Food prices skyrocketed, but even then, almost nothing was available.
Just rice. A few legumes.
That was all.

We couldn't return to our home because the military had not yet withdrawn from our neighborhood. So we went to stay at my grandfather's house for three weeks. When the area around our home was finally accessible, my brothers went to inspect it.

What we found wasn't a home anymore.

The house had been partially destroyed. And then it was set on fire.
They didn't stop shelling. They burned it.
My room was among those consumed by flames.
There was nothing left, not even ashes.

It's hard to put into words.
But the room was *empty*, in the most absolute sense –
as if everything had evaporated.

Still, my brothers went almost daily to see what could be salvaged, clinging to the hope of returning, despite the devastation.
Then, on a Monday morning, two of my brothers – Ahmed, 24, and Mahmoud, 17 – left to inspect the house again. They never came back.

Israeli warplanes bombed them near the house, along with our cousin Hisham, who was 29.
They were killed instantly.

One of their friends who survived the bombing rushed to tell us.
There were no phones. No internet. No working roads.
No way to reach them except through grief.

Now, it feels like I'm reliving the nightmare all over again. The tanks have advanced once more. We've had to leave my grandfather's house. And again, we hear the shells exploding near us – random, terrifying, and constant.

We don't know which missile will end us all.
Or whether it will take just one… and injure the rest.

We have lost so much.
So, so much.

We lost our loved ones.
We lost our home.
We lost our work.
We lost our future.

We lost our dreams.
We lost our universities.
We lost our schools.

Right now, I was meant to be sitting my final exams for the third
semester of my master's degree.

This is not a dystopian fantasy.
This is a small fragment of what I've lived –
in the midst of this unspeakable war.

Our feelings when the war resumed on March 18, 2025

Batol Nabeel Alkhaldy

The night the war returned was a night of tragedy.
Missiles once again rained down on the heads of innocent people, and
　　the sounds – those terrifying, inhuman sounds – cannot even be
　　described.

Still, I told myself, *this won't last long.*
There's an agreement, witnessed by powerful nations – surely Israel
　　won't be able to keep fighting.

But the truth hit harder than any missile:
No one moved for us.
No one acted.
And the fighting came back, fiercer than before.

We hadn't even caught our breath from the last war.
We had just started to dream again, to plan for a future we hoped
　　would be more beautiful.

But the return of the bombs shattered those dreams into pieces.
I don't understand how the whole world remains silent,
　　lips sealed shut.

Why?

We're not asking for luxury.
We're not searching for perfect lives.

We just want something simple –
to wake up to the sound of birds instead of warplanes,
to eat a meal without wondering if it will be our last.

We are children of war.
Every day we live with memories soaked in pain.
And yet,
despite everything,
we still dare to dream –
dreams, not nightmares.

Sometimes, I wonder:
Will the days always be like this?
Is misery our fate, written into our lives until death?

But then I remind myself:
This world is not the end.
Every story has a sequel.
And there is always hope
Because there is a God who sees this world.

When the Voice is Targeted: A Testimony Under Fire About Hasan Aslih

Dalal Sabbah

In the chaos of daily death – when a word can carry more weight than a bullet – Hasan Aslih held his camera like a soldier holds his rifle: not to kill, but to bear witness. In the ongoing war on Gaza, where the sky forecasts only delayed funerals, Hasan was one of the few who didn't sleep, didn't flee, and didn't hide behind silence. He faced terror with unwavering focus and a steady lens.

Hasan Abd al-Fattah Muhammad Aslih, known as Abu al-Abed, was born on December 18, 1987, in Khan Younis, southern Gaza. He began his journalism career in 2009 and rose to become one of Gaza's most prominent field reporters – with a powerful digital presence. He wasn't just reporting the news; he was the eyes of the people and the lens of a land that spoke in blood and rubble.

Hasan ran one of the most followed news channels on Telegram. His platform became a trusted field source for both international media and ordinary people seeking unfiltered truth. Through thousands of images and videos, he built a vast archive of Gaza's pain and resistance – created under the constant threat of erasure: the erasure of life, and of memory.

As a freelance photojournalist, Hasan collaborated with major international media outlets, including CNN and the Associated Press. Since October 7, he had been documenting the horrors unfolding in Gaza with unwavering commitment. He wasn't just a witness – he was a memory keeper, a historian recording from within the fire.

In a reality where journalists have become direct targets, the camera is no longer a shield – it is now an indictment that carries a death sentence. Hasan was not randomly targeted; he was deliberately silenced as part of Israel's systematic policy during the war: the elimination of witnesses to the truth. His assassination was not the first but part of a long, bloody pattern of targeted killings of Palestinian journalists – in their homes, in tents, in cars, and even in hospital beds.

On April 7, 2025, while stationed near Nasser Hospital in Khan Younis, the journalists' tent – meant to be a last refuge – was directly hit by an Israeli airstrike. Hasan sustained severe injuries, losing two fingers and suffering extensive burns. He narrowly escaped death when fellow journalist Tamer Keshta carried him through the flames on his back – a moment that captured friendship defying death and an unbreakable spirit of resistance.

But miracles do not repeat themselves.

At dawn on Tuesday, May 13, 2025, as Hasan lay in a hospital bed in the burns unit at the Nasser Medical Complex, the Israeli drone returned to finish what the first missile had not. It targeted the third floor of the hospital, directly hitting the section where Hasan lay helpless. He was martyred in his bed, burned beneath the rubble – in a double crime: the murder of the wounded, and the murder of the witness.

Tamer Keshta, still camped near the hospital, recalled:
"I heard a massive explosion shake the place. Flames were rising from the third floor, where Hasan was being treated. When we reached him, his body was buried under debris… there was nothing left but ashes."

Hasan was targeted twice, but the second strike carried a message: the camera is more dangerous than the rifle. Exposing the crime is itself a crime in the eyes of the perpetrator.

Hasan left behind a living archive of images and sound – a screen that still displays the truth they tried to bury. He left behind a grieving wife and four children – a boy and three girls – too young to understand what it means to be a journalist in Gaza, or why even a camera warrants a death sentence.

Hasan Aslih was not just another name on the list of the martyred. He was the memory of a people, the voice of a bleeding city, and a lens that kept recording even as it was extinguished beneath the rubble. Behind every missile, there was a picture taken moments before, a clip that documented pain before it disappeared, and a lens that etched into history that truth does not die, even when assassinated twice.

His assassination – first during coverage, then during treatment – places Israel in front of a dual crime: the targeted killing of a journalist, and the violation of medical neutrality. This was not merely an attack on a man, but a deliberate attempt to silence the voice, blur the image, and erase memory from the world's eyes.

Targeting journalists is the assassination of truth. It sends a message: "We don't want witnesses to the crime." But what the executioner fails to understand is this: the lens that captured truth lives on in every conscience, and the word written in the heart of fire cannot be erased, even by blood.

The children of Gaza under the rubble

Raghad Izaat Hammouda

In a crowded neighborhood of Gaza, where houses stand so close they seem to cling to one another for protection from the relentless bombings, lived ten-year-old Laila with her small family. She would wake to the dawn call to prayer, opening her eyes to sunlight filtering through bullet holes in the kitchen wall. In the corner of her tiny room hung her drawings – of olive trees and a sea she'd only ever seen in dreams. Her little brother Youssef played with his patched rag doll, giggling as their mother, Umm Youssef, made shadow puppets in the faint candlelight.

"Baba, when will we go back to school?" Laila would ask as they ate dry bread with olive oil.

"Soon, my love, when the war stops…" Abu Youssef would answer hoarsely, his hands trembling as he tuned their old radio, searching for news of a ceasefire.

One bitter winter night, hunger sat heavily at their table. Umm Youssef could no longer hide her tears as she rationed their remaining food: "Eat slowly – we don't know when aid will come."

Suddenly, the electricity cut out. Air raid sirens wailed like starving wolves. Laila trembled as warplanes roared overhead like endless thunder.

"Hide under the stairs!" Abu Youssef shouted.
But time had run out.

The missile struck the outer wall, reducing their home to rubble. Laila felt herself drowning in darkness, the air thick with dust and screams. She heard Youssef's faint whimper: "Laila… I'm scared!" She crawled toward him, but twisted rebar had impaled her leg. The smell of blood mixed with gunpowder. Her mother's screams – "Save my children!" – were swallowed by the wreckage.

When Laila opened her eyes, the world had turned upside down. She saw her father's hand – still wearing that worn wedding ring – protruding from the debris. She crawled toward it, her knees grinding into broken glass, until she saw his body severed at the ribs, intestines coiled around their last Eid photo frame. His face, turned toward where Umm Youssef had stood with baby Ahmed, was frozen in a silent scream.

Blood was everywhere. Arterial spray had painted grotesque patterns on the walls.

Youssef's sunflower overalls were now just red fabric beneath a concrete slab. Only his tiny sandal remained – his toes still curled from when he'd kicked it off while playing.

Something warm dripped down Laila's neck. A piece of brain matter clung to her headscarf. Looking up, she saw her mother's braid – the one she had woven that very morning – swinging perfectly intact from the ceiling fan.

Then – a sound.

Beneath her father's corpse, eighteen-month-old Ahmed gasped for air. His skull was visibly dented, one eye swollen shut.
As Laila pulled him free, his tiny fingers smeared their father's blood across her cheek.

"La… la…" he gurgled – half-remembering their mother's lullaby.

At Al-Shifa Hospital, where gangrene and disinfectant choked the air, Laila watched a nurse stitch a child's scalp without anesthesia.
"His brain is exposed!" someone shouted.
"Next!" barked a doctor, his scrubs stiff with dried blood.

Clutching Ahmed to her chest – his breathing growing wetter by the minute – Laila took in the horrors:
A girl cradling her brother's severed arm.
An old man drinking urine from an IV bag.
A newborn wailing beside its dead mother.

A month later, in a UN tent, Laila opened her notebook with hands still stiff from her family's dried blood:

Dear Youssef,
Today I saw a boy with your laugh.
I followed him for blocks until his mother called the police.
Ahmed doesn't cry anymore. I think he forgot how.
Love,
Your killer (because I didn't hold you tightly enough).

This isn't just a story.
As you read these words, dozens of Lailas remain buried under Gaza's rubble.

Hundreds of Ahmeds breathe through collapsed lungs.

And thousands of sunflowers will never bloom.

Gaza's children carve their stories into concrete with bare fingernails – begging the world to listen before the last whisper fades.

Gaza bleeds every day but refuses to die –
because her children carry something stronger than bombs:
Memory.

I Buried the Future Too Soon

Nour Ahmed Almajaida

The emotions I'm experiencing are fear and uncertainty.
I don't even know if I'm afraid of death itself or not.
The idea of dying doesn't scare me – we're all going to die one day.
But what *does* scare me is losing all my friends, my family,
    anyone I love – because of this war.

I can't hold the memories without pain.
Sometimes, it hurts more to have the memory when the
    people you made it with are no longer there.
I'm afraid of being alone after the war – of surviving,
    but coming back to nothing.
Will I find my house when I return?
Will I even return?
Will I end up spending the rest of my life here?
Will I have to give up everything I ever hoped for?
Not knowing when this will end, or what will happen next,
    or even if I'll survive until then, fills me with anxiety.

My thoughts are consumed by the future.
I think about the dreams I once had – how so many of them now feel
unreachable, like they belonged to another version of me.
I wonder if the life I imagined will ever exist.

Sometimes I think of my friend who died in the war.
I found out far too late.
I still carry guilt for that.
And often, I wonder if someone else I know has died – someone I
    haven't heard from – without me even knowing.

The hardest thing right now is coping with all these changes.
Coping with the people I'm stuck with, with being home 24/7,
    seeing the same faces every day.
And honestly, most of the time, I hate it.

My top priority right now?
To live in peace until the day I die.
I want a fresh start – a new life, in a new place, with new everything
Somewhere far from here.

I want to live freely, fully, without fear of what tomorrow will bring.

And honestly?

I have no idea how I'm going to make that happen.

Dreams Beneath the Rubble

Aya Khaled Al-Jouran

Hello,

My name is Aya Khaled Al-Jourani. I am 19 years old and live in Gaza, Palestine. I study English at Al-Azhar University.

This war has turned my life upside down. I lost three of my sisters and their innocent children – they were torn to pieces, and we couldn't even bury them. The pain of that loss will never leave me.

Before the war, I dreamed of traveling, learning, and developing my skills in drawing and translation. I lived in a beautiful home and had a peaceful life. Today, I have no home, no safety, and sometimes not even food to eat.

My dreams were buried under the rubble. I now live with fear every day, not knowing if I'll live to see tomorrow. But despite everything, I still dream of a better future.

We, in Gaza, love life. We are not just headlines – we are students, artists, and families. We deserve to live in peace. I miss the simple things: laughter, safety, hope.

Even after losing so much, I still love Gaza. I still hold on to my Palestinian identity. This war took everything from me – but not my will to live, or my hope.

All I want is to live without fear and to one day achieve the dreams I once held close to my heart.

An Unfinished Song

Obay Jouda

The night felt like any other since Israel's 2014 assault. At 10 p.m., my entire family had gathered in my grandparents' house, seeking a false sense of safety amidst the chaos consuming our land. My mother was making tea, while my father and uncles tried to distract themselves with a game of cards.

In the background, Om Kalthoum's voice floated through the air, singing: *"Now I have a rifle... to Palestine they've taken me with you."*

Suddenly, the music was shattered. A bomb struck our neighbor's house, ripping apart what little normalcy we had managed to preserve. If that moment were captured in slow motion, you'd see a blinding yellow flash – like daylight at 10 a.m. – followed by a deafening explosion that shook the earth. The walls trembled violently, possessed by fear. Glass shattered. Children screamed. Women cried out.

My father and uncle rushed out to see what had happened. But we all knew. Their home had become a tomb.

Years later, I found myself revisiting that moment, drawn again to Om Kalthoum's song. I replayed it, listening carefully. It began with a bombing. Just like my life. I waited for the blast to come again, but it didn't. The next line said: *"Twenty years searching for a home and an identity."*

Now, I am twenty years old. Still searching.
So I ask: when will this song end?

A Cry from the Neck of the Bottle: Questions in a Time of Turmoil

by Abd Alaziz M. Ismail

To my brothers and beloved ones in God,

I share with you today something of what I have learned and lived in
this life, carrying questions that weigh heavy on the soul and drive
us to deep contemplation.

Why all this suffocation? Why this paralyzing helplessness that
surrounds us?

Is it our destiny to remain silent, unmoved, as chaos tears through
every corner of our lives?

They describe our condition in Gaza, amidst the raging war, as having
reached "a bottleneck."

Sometimes they whisper to us of patience, as if relief must surely be
born from the womb of suffering.

But let us revisit these expressions.

Have we truly reached the neck of the bottle? And is this bottle
we speak of just any bottle? Or is it one made of stone,
with the narrowest neck in all of history?

Perhaps there is no bottle at all.

Perhaps we, humanity, invented it.

We named it so, and gave it this unyielding hardness.

Had we only paused to reflect, we might have stopped it from
becoming a hardened bottle.

We could have kept it soft, elastic – capable of bending,
resisting rigidity and weight.

Are we truly in the throes of a "difficult birth"?

Or is this a process that can only lead to a torn womb
and a child inevitably stillborn?

I pose these questions because they are at the core of our dilemmas –
and dilemmas, in turn, enrich our understanding and give rise to
scattered truths.

It is our right to question, and to share our questions, so that we might
consult one another as a collective humanity in search of truth –
even if it is bitter – for it may hold the key to our salvation.

Many of our daily struggles stem from disturbances – or rather, from our failure to expose and confront the disturbances around us.

We have allowed the disturbed to roam freely through our lives.

And these are not people content to confine their disorder to themselves – they spread it like a contagion, infecting even the smallest particles of existence.

Just like those who use bombs to massacre unarmed civilians in Gaza.

These bombs merely continue the work of their launchers, transferring their internal chaos to the bodies of civilians – spreading what I call the "spirit of the devil": suffocation, breathlessness, scarcity, hunger, and terrifying fear.

Everyone runs – panicked – as if we are living the horrors of Judgment Day.

All of this unfolds because we have not given enough attention to those spreading their disorder.

We give great attention to our physical measurements, observing how some particles in nature exist in balance and others in constant turbulence.

Through measurements and experiments, we are able to either suppress unstable states that could lead to explosions, or adapt ourselves to avoid such outcomes, or even intervene to prevent detonation altogether.

But why have we not given the same care to the disturbed individuals themselves – those who can ignite chaos and spread their infection to the missile's particles, which in turn spread it to the devastated people of Gaza?

I have seen with my own eyes the spread of the "spirit of the devil" wherever hardship, suffering, and pain take root.

I do not say this to evoke pity, but to begin a consultation – a human dialogue – as beings striving for evolution, peace, and the betterment of this Earth.

We must come to a full realization: our minds compel us to stop such wars, to deny them any chance to erupt.

We must outwit them, just as we seek to outwit the physical particles of nature, in order to halt this madness.

The people of Palestine in Gaza have endured what no rational mind
    can bear – like trying to compress an elephant into a box no larger
    than half a cubic meter.
Perhaps these pressures have given rise to new ideas within us, have
    reshaped our understanding of life, of happiness, of wealth,
    and of peace of mind.
But at the same time, they have taken so much from us, and have not
    granted us the time to put into practice what we have learned.

A day in the war of extermination

Maria Abd Alkareem Mohammed Alhawajri

One ill-fated morning we awoke to the screams of one of our relatives
who lived nearby. The brutal warplanes of the occupation had attacked
them without mercy. Some were martyred. Others survived, bleeding
as they witnessed the catastrophe unfold before their eyes.

Moments passed, and then the indiscriminate shelling began, one
house after another. Ours was among those struck. Ash blanketed every
corner of our home. We couldn't see one another. We were calling out
each other's names, desperate to know: *Was everyone still alive? Had
we lost a loved one?*

But praise be to God – everyone was safe.

The shelling continued, relentlessly. We tried to gather our belongings,
but the scene was terrifying. We hid in the bathroom, hoping it would
be safer than the rest of the house, since it was built of strong concrete,
while the rest of the home was made of fragile asbestos sheets.

We waited and waited for the bombing to stop.

Suddenly, the silence took over. Seizing the moment, we ran. Outside,
a woman lay sprawled on the ground, her limbs torn apart, right in
front of our doorstep. We tried to lift her, to help, but we couldn't.
We ran without stopping, hoping to escape the nightmare.

We managed to find shelter in a nearby school and spent a difficult night there. We lay on the cold floors outside the classrooms, as the place was overcrowded with displaced families. We had no blankets to cover our frail bodies.

As the darkness faded and dawn broke, a massive explosion shook the area near the school.

Then we heard the sounds of tanks approaching.

Bombs began to fall upon us again.

This became our reality throughout the day.

Later, we were ordered to evacuate the school – without any men or young boys to accompany us. Only women and children. Our legs trembled. We rushed forward, only to find tanks in front of us. We kept walking – on and on – for long distances.

At times we lost one another and would break down in tears, trying desperately to reunite.

"Where is my brother? Where is my brother?" a young girl screamed.

Other times, one of us would collapse from exhaustion.

Eventually, we reached another school.

But we had no idea what had become of our men.

The Flurries of War and Life's Hope

Ola Abdullah Suleiman Sheikh Al-Eid

On that cold night, the twelve of us huddled in a single room – so tight it seemed to suffocate us more than protect us. We thought of it as the "safe room" – no glass windows that could shatter, no sharp objects that might turn into deadly shrapnel. As if its silent walls could shield us from the madness of the night and the screaming sky.

We turned off the lights and lay down in silence, trying to outwit the fear hiding in our breaths.

For six months, we had been sleeping in that same room – sharing it, wrapping ourselves in its fragile hope. Twelve bodies, each huddled into a corner they believed to be safer than the rest. But they were all just corners of the same room, like a small prison we were enduring together.

There, in the darkness, each of us carried a quiet longing in our chest – waiting for just one sign of peace to lift the weight pressing on our lungs, to allow us to move freely again, to save us from the sleepless cries of night and the daylight shrouded in unending terror.

We were trapped – between the walls and the panic – trying to find in our stillness a glimmer that might scatter the darkness of war. But it was only a room… a fragile shelter.

The clock struck midnight. But its chime wasn't like other nights. It wasn't just the clang of metal – it was a jolt that pierced the heart, followed by the buzz of warplanes crowding the sky like phantoms devouring all in their path.

Then came the bombing – sudden and savage – as if the sky itself had exploded over our heads. The house shook to its core, as though its very heart trembled alongside ours.

The explosions came one after another – merciless, relentless. The night seemed determined to pour out all its madness in one breath. The planes circled above, leaving no moment of silence. They howled, they roared, they tore through the air – painting death across the sky.

And then we heard them… sounds not of this world, but of a world bleeding.

Women wailing. Children screaming. Cries for help, swollen with despair.

These weren't coming from nearby homes. They echoed from loudspeakers on the planes themselves.

"Don't go outside!" my father shouted.

"This is a trick… they're hunting our souls."

Then came the gunfire – random, indiscriminate.

And then, whispers in the dark:
– "Are you all okay?"
– "Turn off your phone screens."

– "No internet… no electricity… no news. Just the confusion of what's coming – unknown and unseen."
– "Be ready. We might have to leave the house at any moment."
– "I need to go to the bathroom."
– "It's at the end of the hallway, by the window – under a drone that never leaves."

In a sudden flash, a small drone slipped through the open guest room window like a ghost gliding down from the sky. We hadn't heard it approach. But suddenly, the room lit up with an eerie blue glow, flickering across the trembling walls.

Someone whispered: "Don't move… stay still."

What followed weren't minutes – they were lifetimes.

Each second felt like standing on the edge of an abyss, unsure if it would swallow you whole or grant you one more chance to survive.

And then… morning came.

The sky calmed. The drones stopped circling. The bombing ceased.

A strange silence settled – but this time, it wasn't terrifying.

It was a truce-like silence, as if the world had decided to give us one moment of rest.

We stepped out onto the balcony, and life slowly began to return.
There was the greengrocer, opening his modest stall.
There was the man pushing his cart, selling bread.
Little by little, the city began to breathe again.

And life, in its smallest forms, returned.

And I, too, returned – to who I was.

A volunteer.

Moving from one shelter to another.
Helping the displaced.
Distributing blankets.
Recording the names of families.
Tracing with my heart – before my pen – a humble path toward hope.

The Famine in Gaza

Randa Zakaria Al-Basaina

The famine in Gaza is one of the most painful humanitarian crises in the world today. Thousands of families – especially children and women – are living without enough food or clean water. Many eat only once a day. Others go an entire day without eating at all. Malnutrition has left countless children thin, weak, and unable to grow properly.

This famine is not the result of nature. It is man-made – caused by war, siege, and destruction. Gaza has been under blockade for years, making it nearly impossible for food, medicine, and clean water to enter. Trucks carrying aid are often delayed or turned away. Farms, bakeries, shops, and food stores have been bombed. Even the sea is no longer safe for fishermen, making fresh fish and vegetables scarce.

In many homes, there is no electricity. Without refrigeration, food spoils quickly. Cooking is difficult, as gas and supplies are limited. Mothers do everything they can to feed their children, often going hungry themselves so their little ones can eat.

Hospitals are overwhelmed. Some babies have died due to a lack of baby formula. Patients receive little to no food. Doctors and nurses continue their work with courage, but they, too, are in desperate need. Hunger is making people sick – not only physically, but mentally and emotionally.

Yet, amid this suffering, the people of Gaza remain strong. They support one another. Neighbors share what little they have. Families hold onto hope. They pray, they endure, and they continue to show kindness even in the darkest moments.

The world must not turn away. We must speak out. We must tell the truth of what is happening. Governments and organizations must send food, water, medicine, and essential aid. But above all, the war must end. Only peace can stop the hunger and suffering.

One day, I hope Gaza will be a place of peace, safety, and joy. I hope children will grow up strong, attend school, play freely, and never go hungry again. Every human being deserves dignity – and the people of Gaza are no exception.

Islamic University before ▼

Islamic University after ▼

I Write Because the World Is Deaf

Rawan Marwan Omar Matar

I never imagined that writing would become my only means of expressing the rage and screams trapped inside me – not because I chose it, but because the world refuses to hear us, or perhaps chooses not to. In Gaza, we don't tell stories for leisure; we tell them to survive, to help us make sense of what is happening around us. The burden is heavy, and the pain runs deep.

Here in Gaza, we struggle just to stay alive, as if this is no longer our own land. We no longer recognize our streets – the destruction has erased their once-beautiful features. Gaza is now drenched in blood, grief, and sorrow. The people are wounded, broken, lost – their faces covered in dust and burdened by exhaustion. Many have reached the brink of madness under the relentless pressure.

How are we expected to endure such horrors? Bombs fall from every direction. We live in constant fear of losing our loved ones. Homes have vanished, friends are gone, and we cling to those who remain, terrified they might be next. We face terrifying challenges alone: starvation, and the painful inability to feed our children.

In Gaza, there is no longer a distinction between rich and poor – we are all hungry. We say," Hunger knows no mercy," and this truth alone could ignite another civil war. We find ourselves trying to protect our families even from the anguish of our own people.

The occupation deliberately deprives us of medical care. Attacks on hospitals have made it easier for us to die. Overcrowded wards, lacking supplies or tools to treat the wounded, have brought death closer than ever.

Massacres repeat themselves everywhere. The screams, the blood, the brutal scenes of injuries – we have been living with them for two years. What's happening now is either that we have become numb to fear, or that our emotions have grown cold from all we have endured, leaving no space to process another tragedy.

We no longer recognize ourselves. We hold onto happy memories as if we are locked inside a sealed room, far away from this world.

These memories distract us from the harsh reality – they bring us brief moments of comfort, soothe our sorrowful existence, and gently push us to keep living just a little longer.

I am nothing but a precious soul who once had everything – my family and I lived in safety and dignity. But the days turned against us, stripping us of all we had, making us forget who we are. Yet we have had enough. Haven't we endured enough of this genocide? Haven't we carried its burden for long enough? Isn't it time to stop these massacres?

Let the world rise up against this injustice. Let your voice be heard – for we can no longer bear more tragedies. Stop this monstrous genocide, and do not let the world grow numb to the scenes of mass killing, as if it were a daily routine.

Tell it louder. Tell it raw. Exaggerate, if you must – because the world hasn't even tasted a fraction of our truth. It hasn't caught the scent of burning bodies, hasn't heard the full scream of a mother clutching her dead child. Humanity is asleep. So shout it, stretch it, paint it in fire – until even closed eyes are lit by the truth.

Filled with gray

Reem Alaa Khalel Al-Astal

We are followed by words of support and condolences, wrapped in phrases of resilience – as if bare letters could stop our inevitable fate from bowing to a treacherous force. Only those attacked in the blackest hours of night understand the meaning of peace. Only those trapped in a paralyzed land know what it means to lose hope.

Here, because they are *from here,* the living walk like the dead – ghosts of suffering drifting through broken streets. There is no place untouched by ash and ruin. No soul without a painful past, a helpless present, and a future too uncertain to imagine.

Sure, life exists for those beyond the walls – but not in Gaza, under grey skies. Here, we face impossible choices: die at home or die outside. Survive, or pretend to.

Even if you escape death and destruction, you won't outrun famine, displacement, humiliation, and shame.

Our children have lost their childhood. One asks the other, *"Where is our home?"*
The reply is as expected: *"There – in that pile of rubble."*

They whistle when they hear jets overhead. They flinch but do not panic when explosions echo – because they know. They are not ignorant of the truth.

There is nothing more heartbreaking than hearing them talk – about rising food prices, about dreams of a meal that might quiet their hunger. Worse still, they speak of their suffering using political terms – children, forced to learn the language of injustice.

You may stay in your home, but visions strike you: the cracked ceiling collapsing, the agony of a friend or relative torn apart by bullets or bombs, the image of a child who died of hunger.
What does it feel like to live under the rubble?

Will I die of fear in the dark before I feel a thing?
Will they find me easily, or will I be left behind – lifeless and forgotten?
Will my body have a name, or become an unknown corpse?
Is there anything left to stop this ongoing torment?

It is beyond belief. And yet – even if you believe –
    it will not make you feel what we feel.
You will not feel that shiver of fear at the sound of a drone.
You will not hear the cries for help from beneath the debris.
You will not lose your family one by one.
You will not scramble daily to feed your hungry children.
You will not be displaced from your home to a tent, from north to south.
You will not wait for a miracle to pull you out of this.

You will not understand what I'm living.

Million Broken Hearts

Rasha Essa Mohammed Abo Shirbi

It's painfully heartbreaking to think about the days we once called ordinary, the calm, joyful days filled with laughter, before the Israeli occupation declared war on our lives. We had no idea what was coming.

We were forced into the unknown, displaced without warning. What we're enduring now is unbearable.

My home – the walls that held our childhood, the place where we spent lifetimes making memories, where we felt safe, warm, and whole, is now buried under ash. Gone. Unrecognizable.

I can't forget the day we left, broken-hearted and tearful, believing we'd return. Believing we'd live again, peacefully.
But even hope betrayed us, and left us begging and pleading because home is no longer home. Becoming refugees, strays of fate, was already too much to endure.

When you see your warm home, your safe haven, reduced to dust, you learn what real patience means.

When someone you love dies – your brother, your cousin, your grandmother – you understand what it costs.
When you're displaced to a place that resembles everything but a home, living a life that feels hollow – you hold on to patience like it's the only thing left.

I'll never forget the fear they forced into us. How I felt when my house was targeted. The displacement. The helplessness. The hunger. The annihilation. We've been starved for months, denied medical care, stripped of water, and left to survive in the ruins.

I've been separated from my mother, who's abroad. My heart aches for her. I miss her more than words can say.

Some days we eat. Other days, we barely manage a single meal. The conditions here are unbearable. The air is thick with disease, the streets overflow with garbage. This place is suffocating. And if you fall ill, there's no proper care – because the occupation has destroyed every hospital we once had.

Still, we believe.

We believe in Allah, and that belief keeps us standing.
Even when we don't understand, we trust that His mercy is greater than our pain. That He won't forsake her, and He will give us more than we ask for. That with hardship comes ease.

Sometimes, I sit alone and remember the good old days, when laughter filled the halls of our house, when joy was ordinary, when the days passed gently. Those days are gone. Bombed. Buried. Reduced to rubble with no features and ashes, along with the memories we once lived in.

When we heard the news that our home was gone, it felt like a knife to
    the heart. I sobbed until there were no tears left.
I wish I could turn back time, live every moment as if it were my last.

Our lives have been shattered in ways that feel beyond repair. But
    even in all this sorrow, we stayed strong. Not because we are
    unbreakable, but because we have faith.
We believe Allah is closer to us than our own heartbeat.
And we will keep holding on – tight – to hope.

Because we were not created to break,
but to rise.
To fight.
To awaken – despite the darkness around us.

Deprivation of Everything

Adiba Ghassan Khader

Our suffering in Gaza is embodied in painful, daily scenes of loss
    and deprivation.

We live under the constant threat of airstrikes – sudden attacks
    that do not distinguish between a child, a woman, or the elderly.
The constant displacement and destruction. Homes reduced to rubble
Entire neighborhoods flattened. Families forced to move from
    place to place, with no safe shelter.

And above it all – siege.

A crippling blockade has caused severe shortages of food, medicine, electricity, and clean water, lasting for years with no relief in sight.

The future is a blur.
Children are denied education. Youth are left with no jobs, no opportunities, and dreams buried beneath the ash.

Hospitals are overwhelmed, desperately lacking medicine and medical equipment.
Thousands have been martyred, while medical staff work under unbearable pressure.

Schools have been bombed or turned into shelters for displaced families. Thousands of students are cut off from their education, trying to learn under impossible emotional and physical conditions.

Shops are shuttered.
Even bread and clean water are hard to come by.
People wait in endless lines for fuel or food, haunted by the constant sound of drones overhead.

Travel for treatment, for education, or simply to survive has become a distant dream.

Our suffering in Gaza is not just statistics.
It is real stories of souls trying to hold on despite everything.

In Gaza, we are not just living through a military war.
We are living through a war on every detail of life.

The Weight of Silence

Samah Mustafa Yousef Bashir

Silence in Gaza is not peace.
It is the silence of empty chairs at the breakfast table.
Of phones that no one answers.
Of streets once echoing with children's laughter – now shy beneath their footsteps.

I used to think silence was gentle, like dawn or falling snow.

But here, it feels like heavy waiting, waiting for the next name to be added to the list of the dead.

Every morning, I pass by the school I once studied in.
Its windows are shattered, its door dangling like a loose wire.
Yet the flag still flies.
Sometimes I wonder – has it grown tired of standing in the wind too?

I saw a child writing on the wall with chalk.
I walked closer.
He had written: *"My father promised to take me to the sea."*
Signed with a single letter – perhaps his name, or maybe just his hope.

There is a kind of sorrow that doesn't cry.
It seeps into the way my mother stirs the spoon though there's nothing to cook,
the way my brother puts on his school uniform every morning, even though school has stopped,
the way we sit at the table, trying not to count who's missing.

And yet, in this silence we resist.
Not with weapons, but with presence.
With stories.
With the courage to write, and to remember.

I write because silence must not win.
I write because if the world forgets us, I will not forget myself.
And if my words reach even one heart beyond this siege, then I have broken through the wall.

We may not have much
but we have the truth,
and the courage to carry it in every sentence,
every breath,
every day we survive.

Gaza under attack

Hadeel Waleed Abu Tawela

What we live through in Gaza today is beyond the imagination of
anyone outside this genocide.
Even though social media has worked tirelessly to share our reality,
the picture remains incomplete, and our voices still go unheard
by the world.

You can't spend an entire day outside your home – if you do, you know
you'll return eventually, even if it's just to the rubble.
The stones of our homes still bear witness to our joy, our childhoods,
our memories, and the comfort we once had.

But tents are no homes.
They are unliveable – scorching under the sun by day,
freezing through the night.
We went from a spacious two-story house to a small tent
shared by the whole family. The tent is the bedroom,
the living room, and the kitchen all in one.

Food is scarce.
Even those who once could afford to buy are now helpless
in the face of skyrocketing prices.
You stare at vegetables you can't afford and find yourself
wishing for death just to escape the hunger.
We survive on canned food, most of it expired, causing stomach problems,
exhaustion, and constant fatigue. There are no alternatives.

Drinking water is undrinkable.
Bathwater is worse.
Sewage runs through the streets, spreading disease and bacteria.
People's health is deteriorating.

And we cannot forget the massacres.
The Israeli occupation continues to kill civilians and entire Palestinian
families without regard – whether they are children, women, or
the elderly.
They drop missiles on tents that offer no protection. One targeted tent
sends shrapnel flying through the neighboring ones, increasing the
number of martyrs and wounded.

Gaza's hospitals are out of service, crushed by the lack of resources,
   medicine, and medical equipment.
The wounded wait for death. Their conditions worsen while the world
   watches in silence.

Here, the martyr is the only one who survives this holocaust.
He dies, and no longer has to wonder what comes next.
He doesn't fear the next round of airstrikes.
He doesn't wait for the end of the siege.
He is already in paradise.

2024

Nour Mohammed Abusultan

The year began with an eviction notice – another displacement.
We left Nuseirat for Rafah, our seventh stop on the journey of
   homelessness.

A house without windows took us in.
We were drowned by the first drops of rain, and the harsh cold
   wrapped around our bones.
One small room held us all – after once feeling that even an entire
   house was too small.
We learned that coexistence was no longer a choice, and that patience
   was the only path forward.

On a barren patch of land, I named it *"Al-Khadraa" – The Green One*
– I keep searching for a seed of hope in the midst of despair.

The clay oven became our companion, reviving memories and
   gathering what remained of us.
It carried the warmth of family, even through the harshest nights.
And from the ashes, a yellow flower bloomed – a tiny sun in the
   darkness – whispering to me that even here, the harshest places
   of all, life could grow.

Transportation is overcrowded. Prices burnt our pockets.

Still, we learned to smile through pain and to live through hardship.
Illness exhausted us. Hospitals denied us basic rights.
Yet faith in healing, in endurance was our quiet strength.

And through it all, I studied.
I held my books tightly, even when dreams felt suffocated,
    because the future doesn't wait.

I look in the mirror and barely recognize myself
A tired face, eyes heavy with sorrow.
Still, I go on.

My little sister grows before my eyes, and with her,
    hope of a better future grows too.
Even with rising prices, we celebrated the smallest joys, a cake, a
    cinnamon roll, turning emptiness into lasting memories.

2024 stood between pain and hope, between loss and resilience.

It taught me that no matter how harsh life becomes, there is always a
    flicker of light.

My resilience was my strength.
My hope, my weapon.

And I still believe
that tomorrow will be more beautiful,
and that flowers can bloom from ash.

No humanitarian in Gaza

Waad Hamdi Mahmood Allaham

Let's speak, for a moment, about the tragedy of a small place in this
    vast world – Gaza.
A city that has become the epicenter of sorrow in a world that remains
    silent.
Gaza holds thousands of heartbreaking stories, and one in particular
    stays with me.

A man once went to get flour to feed his hungry children.
He entered what they call a "humanitarian zone," though in truth,
 it was a death trap for Palestinians.
After struggling to get that single bag of flour, the Israeli occupation
 forces shot him.
He was killed on the spot beside him, the flour bag soaked in his blood.

And still, many bitter stories continue.
They happen every day, on the bleeding soil of Gaza.

Not Just Numbers: The Story of a Soul Silenced

Hada Mohammed Homaid

In Gaza, people die in the way the world fears most suddenly, senselessly, without warning.

No goodbyes. No time to prepare. And what then? No space in the morgue refrigerators. No coffins. Not even cars left to carry the bodies.

Two years ago, Gaza was a place of unshaken pride and radiant dignity. It was known for the generosity of its people, the beauty of its land, and the endless horizon of its pure blue sea. But today, Gaza is wrapped in the shadows of indiscriminate bombs, stalked by serpents of thick black smoke, steeped in the smell of blood, and haunted by the sounds of hunger and fear.

Gaza today resembles a funeral that never ends. A delayed burial for thousands. The world has grown used to the constant count of martyrs, the wounded, and the displaced. But behind each number is a home that bleeds, weeps, and grieves – a mother mourning her child, a wife without her husband, children with no parents left to hold them.

These martyrs are not statistics. They are not digits in a daily report. They are beloved partners, family, friends.

One of them was my guiding light. My second father. He was not a number, not a footnote in history. He was our soul.

His name was Al-Hassan. He began life with relentless determination. At just 18, he secured a stable job while continuing his academic studies, eventually graduating as a lieutenant. At 21, he married and managed to balance the demands of work, study, and family. His rise continued – he became a major, earned a bachelor's degree in law and police science, and completed postgraduate studies in law.

He was deeply committed to his family visiting his parents daily, caring for his siblings, and giving all his heart to his wife and children. He moved through life quickly and with wisdom, a quiet urgency no one understood until he was martyred.

Al-Hassan never wanted to live as a passive bystander. And he succeeded in that.

Many others, like my brother, had dreams, families, and futures. But fate had its own plan.

They say foul is fair and fair is foul. But I still cannot see the fairness in this fear, or the justice in the suffering we endure.

One truth remains: this life is short. This fragile flame will go out. And when the day of judgment arrives, every tyrant will be held accountable for every drop of innocent blood they spilled.

She

Reem Alaa Khalel Al-Astal

She wished happiness could find a place in her life.
She began to wonder – was it her fault for simply being who she was?
She wasn't dangerous, not important, not even part of anything
    harmful. Just... less than ordinary.
Yet they saw her as a threat – a terrorist, a worthless animal to
    be erased.

Is she just unlucky?
Or is life itself too broken to be worth living?
She walked without direction, without knowing what came next.

She raised her hands, staring at nothing…for nothing.
She couldn't accept becoming so breakable, so paralyzed.
This wasn't the time to play hero. She couldn't save anyone.
     Couldn't even save herself.
Submission felt like the only option. But what kind of life is that
     living like a puppet, dancing to a tune she despises?

She hoped sunlight could heal what they had wounded.
But it was deeper than skin. The scars weren't just visible,
     they were buried in her soul.

Maybe, she thought, a breath of fresh air would make things better.
But how?
When the air is thick with blood and gunpowder.
Would they even care if she paused for a sip of water? Just water.
She once had a beautiful life.
Now, nothing is left.

She had lived in light, full of ambition.
Now... she knows she's been handed a life sentence.

She repeats to herself:
"Stay alive until you cross the line."
"Don't look back."
"Don't make a sound."
"Avoid that leg… that arm."
"A beautiful toy, with no owner."
"A row of ruined cars."
"Was that a man or a woman?"
"Just a body – no bones left to burn."

She prays it ends in the least painful way.
She doesn't care anymore about her teary eyes, trembling hands,
     the numbness spreading through her limbs.
She's left everything behind.

Now she understands what displacement really means.
Homeless, shelterless, starving, not just for food,
     but for the memory of who she was.
For everything she lost.
Scars from the dark remain.

How foolish she was to believe she could return home.

She left pieces of herself there.
Now, how can she prove who she is?
How does she face the humiliation?
She's only running from bad to worse.

She knows now: peace was never promised to her.
And yet… she still wants to try.

She left home for what she thought would be a day, maybe two.
She didn't know it would become two years.
All she ever wanted was life.

But life… passed her by.

Our ambitions are broken and Our dreams are torn

Hanan Yousef Naem Al Shennawi

From the heart of Gaza, I live through destruction, hunger, fear,
    and the collapse of life's basics – no clean water, no clothes, no
    food, no way to study.

I spent sleepless nights studying, working hard to earn admission
    to university. And thank God, I did. It came after so much effort
    and exhaustion.
But just as I was about to chase my dreams, war came
    ripping them apart before my eyes.
My happiness, my determination, my ambition – all gone.
Now I feel like a bird with no wings.
I dream of flying, but I can't. I'm tied down by chains I didn't choose.

We're deprived of everything.
I live in a small tent with my family.
I miss privacy, comfort – even a moment of peace.

The phone I use for online learning isn't mine. It's shared among the
    family, and that makes studying difficult.
I walk far from our tent to find an internet connection and stay up all
    night while the world sleeps, my body weak, hungry, and drained.
    We lack food, vitamins, and any basic nourishment.

Paying university fees is a dream on its own.
My father can barely feed us, let alone cover tuition.
And this, heartbreakingly, puts my education on hold.

We live without safety or stability.
Bombs, fear, and forced displacement haunt us daily.

We lack everything.
But still, we try. We struggle.
And we pray that God will reunite us with our dreams.
I still hope… that dreams can come true.

We are not okay.
We only *pretend* to be okay.

Thank God – for strength, and the will to hold on.

The age of roses and experiences

Doaa Qunno

In what they call *"the flower of my youth"* – the beginning of my
twenties, the age of bloom and becoming – I wished to dissolve, to
vanish. Or perhaps I wished *not* to dissolve, but to be erased – along
with my agony.

Let my body remain, maybe it could serve a purpose.
Perhaps they could burn my clothes to light a fire – one without smoke
     – to cook *nothing* on.
Or maybe my body could become a hearty meal for one of the starving
     animals of my land – creatures we starved when we devoured their
     food, or slaughtered when we devoured them.

Maybe, in my absence, someone will eat better.
Maybe, in my death, someone's ration share will grow larger.

Maybe someone will look at my scattered limbs and
     curse the occupation again.
Maybe I'll be accepted as a martyr – one more name
     in the count that can't be ignored.

Maybe then, the numbers will swell so greatly that the world
can no longer look away.

Maybe then, the International Court of Justice, the UN Security
Council, and all the so-called peacemakers will finally do the job
they were created to do.
Maybe someone, somewhere, will abandon their apathy.

Maybe I'll be the *last martyr* – and the occupation will finally be full,
satisfied after gorging itself on blood.
Maybe then, the death machine will rest.

But how could it rest
when the "benevolent" Arab fuel hasn't run out yet?

The Path of Survival

Ola Abdullah Suleiman Sheikh Al-Eid

Flour is almost gone.
Canned food too.
We survive on one meal a day.
We carry water from far distances and walk even farther to complete
daily tasks that now feel heavier than our bodies can bear.

Life is exhausting, to a breaking point.
Prices outside are fire.
Cash is nearly non-existent.

– "There's a center distributing flour. They say it's cheaper nearby.
Let's walk through the tents and alleyways and ask around – maybe
we'll find canned food at a better price."
– "We'll walk for hours without food… but truly what is our crime?"

On the way, we stopped at a stall with rusted cans.
– "How much for peas and beans?"
– "13 shekels, please."
– "We're a big family. One can isn't enough. We can barely afford
anything… the bank deducts 45% of every withdrawal, and cash itself
is scarce!"

– "Let's keep walking. Maybe we'll find something cheaper."

Half an hour later, still nothing.

Then, we heard it, like the sound of celebration:
– "Aid distribution has started! First come, first served!"
– "Really? Look! That child's carrying a food box!"
– "Hey, kid! How did you get it?"
– "The aid is there, an hour's walk away, maybe more. No vehicles allowed. You have to follow a marked path. If you deviate, they shoot."
– "Do you need ID?"
– "No, but they scan your fingerprint."
– "So… my wife, my kids, and I, we can each get a box?"
– "Yes, as long as you're civilians."
– "We are. Peaceful civilians. Let's go – maybe this is our breakthrough! The famine will end. Prices will drop, right?"
– "Millions are walking like us. Famine has devoured everyone – doctors, scholars, journalists alike."
– "Even market stalls are empty, and what little remains is unaffordable."

An hour and a half of walking.
The road was packed with desperate people hoping for one box to feed their families. Above us, warplanes roared in the sky.

At the checkpoint, soldiers stood – guns raised, mirrored glasses on, watching everyone.

– "We've arrived. Follow the rules. Police are watching. Drones overhead. One mistake could cost us everything."
– "This is the women's path; that's the men's. Let's go."
– "It's the first day. Fewer women here – maybe we'll get through quickly. But how can I carry a heavy box in this state? Hunger makes the impossible seem doable. I could lift a truck if it had food."
– "Look at the number of men! Will they all get aid?"
– "Many women didn't come. They're watching their children or don't know the rules."

A guard tried to reassure us:
– "Don't worry. Inside, there are trucks – enough for more than two million Palestinians."
– "My husband and siblings couldn't come. They missed their chance."

– "This place is organized."
– "Look! People coming out with boxes – men, women, children."

Suddenly, confusion erupted. The soldiers grew tense.

– "There's disorder. The men's line is full – they're pushing into the exit path!"
– "They're starving. They can't wait!"
– "No, they realized the truth. Only 500 boxes are left inside."
– "What now?"
– "Shall we kill the ones breaking order?"
– "The media's watching. If we open fire, our image will suffer!"
– "Hunger is brutal. The people turned on us. We must retreat!"
– "Cover us with drones. Fire in the air!"
– "Retreat! These people are wild, desperate!"
– "They destroyed the scanning devices. The lines are gone!"
– "This is the consequence of repeating words that are contradictory to reality!"
– "Why didn't you prepare aid for tens of thousands? These people haven't eaten in days!"
– "How can you let one group receive aid, while another walks over an hour only to be told: 'It's over, come back tomorrow'?"
– "Of course they won't accept that. Their dignity won't allow it."
– "What happened was catastrophic. One small spark exposed massive failure."
– "The media doesn't know we only had 500 boxes left… Let's spin it."
– "We'll say the people destroyed their own aid source. No one will question us."
– "Let's say they were greedy. That they wanted more than one box each."
– "No one's watching closely, say whatever you want."
– "We're innocent in front of the media. Let the truth stay buried. Tell them we were attacked, despite our generosity."
– "Yes. We're innocent. They're the guilty ones."
– "They're rebels… terrorists. Without the drones covering us, we would've been in danger."

But in truth…

The crowd returned to their tents, empty-handed.
Their hearts heavy

They were only dreaming of one box… to feed their family for two days, to silence their children's cries, to survive a little longer.

But that dream was crushed – under the wheels of indifference, the weight of neglect, and warplanes that filled the sky not to deliver bread – but to suffocate hope.

⁓

In One Moment… My Father, My Dream, My Gaza Was Gone

Abdullah Zaher Al-Holy

Since childhood, I looked up to my father with pride.
He was a police officer – walking with confidence, wearing his uniform
    with dignity and grace.
I dreamed of being just like him.
I told everyone, *"When I grow up, I'll be like my father."*

That dream grew with me.
Every moment spent by his side nourished it.
I imagined standing next to him at the station, wearing the same badge,
    serving people with the same courage and honor.

But in Gaza, dreams are fragile. Nothing is guaranteed.
In a single moment, everything changed.
Bombs shook our home, and fear replaced the warmth in our hearts.
I never imagined that one day, *home* would become a memory.

At 8:30 a.m. on May 19, 2024, Israeli warplanes launched two drones
    targeting my father without warning.
It was the third attempt on his life.
I was sleeping upstairs when my phone wouldn't stop ringing.
Friends and relatives were calling, their voices tense.

One friend asked me to come quickly. His voice was off –
    shaky, unsure.
I rushed to his house, full of dread.
He held my hand tightly, but didn't explain. I kept asking what was
    wrong, but he stayed silent.

As we reached the street beside his home, I saw it – rubble,
 smoke rising.
I just knew: this strike was meant for my father.

And then, I saw his bodyguard – his body torn in half.
That was the moment everything shattered.
My father was there too. The rescue operation began.

Gradually, the awful truth unfolded: my father, the province's
 central intelligence director, had been martyred.

My brothers and I rushed to Al-Aqsa Hospital.
I felt like my soul was slipping away.
The world went dark. I had lost the anchor God once gave me.
I kept praying it wasn't true.

But reality hit harder: I lost my cousins, my aunt's entire family,
 and our home – all in days.
With them, I lost pieces of my soul.

I found myself alone in a place where we once laughed together.
My clear dream was now buried in blood and dust.

Today, I no longer dream of becoming a police officer.
But I still dream.
I speak loudly, telling our story to reflect the tragedy of Gaza.

In a single moment, an entire family's future vanished.
Just moments earlier, they were gathered – laughing, living, hoping.
Then came the strike… and nothing was the same.

Such is the cruel reality of Gaza.

But we find comfort knowing this world is temporary, and that our true
 reunion awaits in Paradise, among the prophets, the martyrs, the
 righteous. What a blessed gathering that will be.

A year and a half into this genocide, the shadow of war still looms,
 creeping into every home, every child's mind, every elder's breath.

Now, death doesn't only come from airstrikes.
It comes from hunger.
From disease.
From cold.
From the slow, agonizing collapse of daily life.

Malnutrition is taking lives.
Diseases are spreading as medicine vanishes and hospitals fall apart –
    while the world watches silently, offering only hollow statements
    we've heard too many times.
Words soaked in neglect.

We have no shelter. No food. No medicine.

Flour has become a dream.
Clean water, a rare treasure.
A simple piece of bread feels like a blessing from another world.

Our children fall asleep to the sound of their empty stomachs.
Mothers pray for death – not for themselves, but so they won't have to
    watch their children suffer anymore.
In Gaza, hunger is not a passing pain,
It is a permanent reality.

It gnaws at our children's bodies.
It suffocates the strong.
It breaks us silently,
Because the world has chosen not to see.

And yet, we resist.

We resist with dignity.
Even in hunger,
We resist.

12 kg

Hada Mohammed Homaid

For the past two years, two years of uninterrupted war, I had neither
the passion nor the will to write. But recently, after seeing the martyrs'
bodies torn to pieces, I thought: I might also be torn to pieces, and no
one may gather what's left of me.

So I decided, at the very least, to gather my thoughts – to put my
feelings into words. Maybe the words will survive. Maybe I won't.

It didn't take deep contemplation. As Gazans, we live in a reality that screams without needing much reflection. One thing dominates: hunger. Hunger is the ruler, the tyrant. It's etched into the faces of every passerby.

We are living through the darkest era in Gaza's history, a time when infants, who should never even know what hunger is, are starving. And though they don't know the word, they feel it – deeply, instinctively, painfully.

Gaza is fading, slowly, step by step, through every imaginable form of suffering, right in front of a world that has gone blind and deaf.

Let's talk, just for a moment, about how Gaza is disappearing.

First: the indiscriminate bombs.

Second: the staggering civilian death toll.

Third: the hunger, the famine, the starvation.

Are those three words enough to carry the weight of what we see? Probably not. So let me describe it.

We were taught in school about something called the food pyramid, the idea that every human needs a variety of foods in balanced portions. But in Gaza, people have stopped asking for variety. Today, all Gazans search only for a single, bare piece of bread. Vitamins and proteins are forgotten dreams. We no longer eat to feel full – we eat to survive.

And even that piece of bread is often soaked in blood.

Our lives are traded for sacks of flour – just enough to feed starving children whose tiny bodies have become dangerously thin, shockingly light.

What about the infants?

Let me say it plainly: they can't breastfeed – their mothers are starving too.

But keep your mind at peace: they're nursing on lentils.

Infant formula, as we all know, has somehow become a threat to "national security," so it's banned from entering Gaza.

The siege spares no one — not babies, not children, not the elderly. Not even animals.

I hate going outside.

It's unbearable to see a child whose bones seem ready to stab through his skin — not his flesh, because there's no flesh left.

And I hate the despair I feel standing before these children.

But my pity isn't for us, the hungry, it's for every so-called "free" person in the world who claims to have dignity and a conscience, yet remains unmoved by the hunger in Gaza.

What are you waiting for?

There's nothing worse that can happen. We've already reached the bottom.

And yet, our hearts, our spirits, and our pride still fly.

Gaza is free.

Gaza is great.

Whether the oppressors accept it or not.

Silent Pain

Yasmeen O

Behind every silence, there is a story — and behind every story, a pain written in bleeding ink.

Not every silence is comforting; sometimes, pain comes quietly,

sneaking into your soul without noise, yet causing unseen chaos.

Here, I will not raise my voice... I will simply write, in a low tone, like the heartbeat of a soul in pain.

When pain lives silently within you, it is not just a passing ache –

it is a sorrow that settles in your depths, suffocating your spirit without sound, piling up in silence.

It is the kind of pain that cannot be told, because words sometimes fail to capture it.

Perhaps it is hunger, loss, or the absence of a homeland...

but in the end, it is a grief that is never declared – carried between the ribs and dwelling in dimmed eyes.

In every war, some die in body, and others die in spirit every single day... silently.

This text is your scream when you searched for your voice and could not find it –

your tear that you locked within when you desperately needed to cry.

Silent pain...

A pain no words can ease, no consolation can soothe.

It is the feeling of betrayal by a deaf world,

a world that sees pain and turns away.

In every corner of the soul: a painful memory, a farewell moment,

or the frozen hunger in a child's eyes.

It is the pain that passes each day as a breaking news headline, then is forgotten.

But it stays alive in the hearts of those who lived it –

beating in the silence, telling a story that will never be broadcast, but is engraved in memory forever.

It is the ache hidden behind the eyes, behind forced smiles, behind long silence that defies explanation.

In war, losses are not limited to bombs and rubble; they seep into the soul.

Some lost their homes, others their families, and some lost themselves while still breathing.

War does not always scream; sometimes it walks quietly –

but leaves behind shattered hearts and souls aching in silence.

Hunger, fear, and waiting... all are wars fought within, growing fierce in a painful, wordless silence.

In war, silence becomes the language of survivors, and tears become a luxury the hungry cannot afford.

No voice rises above the sound of oppression,

no shadow can fill the absence that devours souls.

It is a pain that cannot be written, but lives deep in the spirit.

A pain that makes no sound, but tears you apart.

It is that silent pain… unbearable and unspeakable.

Voices from Gaza: Hunger and Dignity

Hadeel Waleed Abu Tawela

There's a deep ache, a choking pain, when you watch the world
    move on as if nothing is happening, as if we don't exist, as if
    Gaza isn't bleeding.
People elsewhere dine in restaurants, stroll through parks, plan
    vacations, chase dreams, laugh freely, and sleep without fear.

Meanwhile, we are trapped beneath a sky heavy with smoke,
    surrounded by shattered buildings and soaked in the blood
    of our loved ones
All we see is rubble.
All we hear are screams.
All we smell is death.

In Gaza, hunger isn't just a lack of food, it's a weapon.
We are not starving because we are poor.
We are not.

We are a people of dignity, pride, and a fierce will to live.
We have money, but there is nothing to buy.
The markets are empty. The shelves are bare. No vegetables,
    no legumes, not even the simplest grains.
This hunger is manufactured.
Imposed by an occupying force that controls even the air we breathe.

Here, people don't just starve, they're forced to choose between
    humiliation and survival.
Many run after aid trucks, hoping to return with a bag of flour –
    knowing they might not return at all.
These lines are not a gateway to life, but a gamble with death.
Some come back carrying bread.
Others come back carried in white shrouds.

And still, despite everything, we are not just hungry, we are aching.
The real hunger is not in our stomachs, but in our hearts.
Hunger for justice.
Hunger for freedom.
Hunger for a life like any other people on this earth.

What kills us isn't the emptiness of our plates –
It's the emptiness of the world's conscience.

How can the world witness all this, and continue
    as if nothing ever happened?

We are bleeding.
We are starving.
Our voices are smothered.

But our dignity stands tall.

Yes, we are tired –
but we are not broken.
Yes, we are forgotten –
but we are not defeated.

We are not beggars.
We are steadfast.
And we will keep breathing dignity until our last breath,
    until our final moment.

Under the Final Dawn

Marah Alaa El-Hatoum

She stands alone, waiting for a sliver of sunrise, for a new day to begin.
She gazes skyward, lost in thought, whispering her grief to God with a
tear that flickers between hope and shame – wiped gently by the light
of a distant dawn.

She sighs, inhales air laced with gunpowder, and offers the sky a
    fragile smile of gratitude… then lies down to rest.
In the morning, she feels safe.
But the night –
The night terrifies her, chokes her, makes her fear closing her eyes.

Everyone is asleep, or returned to sleep after prayer, in a stillness
    that offers no peace.
She sits on the edge of two faded brown mats, cramped in a space
    barely wide enough for her weary body. She doesn't want to
    wake her children – those sorrow-soaked souls.
She leans her head against the wall, hoping for a dreamless nap.
She looks at them all with a quiet fear – what if this is the last time?
She closes her eyes… to escape the thought.

Her phone rings – suddenly, after a long, solemn silence.
As if it had been waiting for this news to shatter her.

"Your father is dead… he died far away, calling your name,
longing to return."

But it wasn't just that.
It was the weight of heaven and earth crashing together.
Another strike.
Another death with no one held accountable.

The land corners her.
The enemy surrounds her.
Death sits quietly at her door.

The voice of exile bleeds through the speaker, as if the news had
    splattered her face with blood from afar.
No escape.

No strength.

No hope.

Only this silence… facing the occupier with no weapon, no food –
  nothing but a trembling heart.

Then the sky howled.

It struck the earth, ripped open graves, let echoes of the dead pour out.

Soldiers came.

They shook her sleeping children awake for the final time.

They threw them to the ground – again.

Blood painted the bedding red.

She screamed – silently.

Her youngest son clung to life, moaning, eyes wide with pain.

He looked at her and whispered with his gaze:

"Mama… it hurts."

Then he sighed… smiled…

and died.

The enemy looked on – mocking.

One soldier raised a pistol to her temple.

She turned slightly, trying to dodge the bullet –

and saw a man hiding nearby.

She called out to him – softly, brokenly.

The soldiers turned and chased him.

They left her.

But as she turned back – another man approached.

This one held an axe.

Pain never comes alone.

He struck.

She opened her mouth to scream –

but no sound came.

She jolted awake.

Her son was beside her, gently calling her for dawn prayer.

She breathed in relief.

She prayed – this time not out of routine, but with a heart crying:
"O Allah, let this routine last forever. Let this peace stay."

Her husband paced in the dark, searching for a flashlight.
She looked out the window –
A sunrise pierced the darkness.

But then –
A missile.

From far away.
Heading toward them.

She opened her mouth to scream, to beg fate to delay…
But no voice came.

No one answered.

And as the missile fell,
She fell too –
beneath the light of her final dawn.

Osama… a voice that faded before it could truly be heard

Rasha Ismail Musabeh

Since the age of two, his journey with autism began.
He feared the dark.
Whenever the electricity went out and the house fell into silence,
he would cry, searching for safety, for his father's arms.

One evening, the lights suddenly cut off.
He screamed, his voice trembling: *"Dad… Dad!"*
Those were the last words we ever heard from him.
After that, the screams stopped
and with them, Osama's voice fell silent forever.

Today, he is 17.
Still wrestling daily with life.

But war has turned him from a child who once played under the sun into a pale face hiding under a tent soaked in sorrow.

He was displaced.
He lost everything – his garden, his room, his sense of self.
He no longer goes to the bathroom alone.
He wears diapers now – forced into a childhood he never chose.

He cries every day.
He sleeps hungry.
Sometimes, he doesn't eat at all.
Famine makes no distinction – child or adult.
And Osama is just one of thousands of forgotten lives under canvas and dust.

The sounds of drones and missiles haunt him.
Every blast sends him running, hiding his head beneath a blanket – as if the fabric could shield him from death.

And when I look into his blue eyes, I see the questions he cannot ask:

Where is my home?
Where is the garden filled with chirping birds and blooming flowers?
Where is my room, full of toys?
Why did we leave it all behind?
What did I do wrong?

A girl who doesn't give up

Sara Aljayyar

Here I am – an ambitious girl who loves science, photography, reading, and writing. I'm in my early twenties – 22 years old – with big dreams and high hopes. I always strive to become the best version of myself. I am a success story in progress, and I'm proud of every step I've taken.

I had just completed my third year of university, studying English Commerce in a four-year program. I was excited to begin my final year – the year of graduation, the joy every student dreams of. But then the war came.

It stole that joy – he joy of graduating, perhaps the most beautiful of all.

Still, I didn't give up.

I completed my final year under bombardment, through displacement and daily power outages, and I earned the highest grades despite it all. Every time we were forced to flee, I carried my pens and notebooks with me. I studied wherever I could.

I am proud – I finished my fourth year under the most difficult circumstances.

Yes, sometimes I feel sad. I wanted to celebrate graduation like any other student to wear the cap and gown, to feel the applause.
But I remember the verse:
"And perhaps you hate something while it is good for you."
Praise be to God, always.

I still have many dreams. I want to achieve them.
But I need this war to end.

I am still here. I haven't given up.
We want peace. We want this war to stop.

I wake up every day and keep trying.
But it's dangerous. I'm afraid to move around, afraid to attend in-person classes – because the bombing is random.

Still, I continue learning online, because I don't want to waste my time. I refuse to sit in silence.

I am here, from Gaza – my proud homeland.
And all I ask is for the war to stop,
so I can live,
so I can achieve my dreams.

The Question That Haunts Us: When?

Farah Jeakhadib

How strange this life we live is!

What one calls a dream, might be someone else's nightmare. Picture it:

a quiet night under a sky full of stars, your whole family in one room, sharing food, warmth, and fleeting peace. It would've seemed like a beautiful, simple dream had someone told me of it before I lived it.... in a very different way.

Yes, the sky is lit – but not by stars. By warplanes. By flares that steal the night.

And that silence? It's not peace. It's the sound of waiting – for the next explosion that shreds not only bodies, but what's left of our hearts.

Now, my family shares a tent – not a home. A tent that shields us from nothing. Not the biting cold of winter, nor from the burning heat of summer, and worst of all, cannot protect us from the flying shrapnel of death.

We share a piece of bread, if we're lucky. And to get it, someone has to walk out into death and come back – "if they come back."

Our days are no longer about living – they're about "SURVIVING". Food. Water. Medicine. That's all life means here now.

My brother – his eye wounded, his vision slipping away – has been waiting for five months for permission to leave Gaza, just to save what remains of his sight.
Every morning, he wakes up early to go to a place ironically named "Gaza Humanitarian Foundation." A place far removed from anything remotely humane.

You've seen Squid Game, haven't you?

It mirrors our lives exactly.
You must fight, sacrifice, and endure

just to earn a bite of food.
All the while, my parents live with a gnawing fear:
will their son return holding bread –
or be carried back on shoulders, lifeless?

My brother should be in a hospital. Recovering. Eating meals fit for someone healing. But here, even the sick must feed themselves – and their families.

I look up from where I sleep, and I see the sky, not peaceful, not calm, but filled with warplanes.
My mind is flooded with endless questions.
And it's not only the questions, it's the answers that storm me like chains,
binding me, stopping me from understanding
why the world lets this happen.

A war crime –
that's what it was when little Hind Rajab's family was killed in their car. All of them. And she was left alone, whispering to the Red Cross: "Please… come get me. I'm really scared. They're all dead. Please come." Did the soldier think? Even for a second? *Maybe there are children in there?*

Another war crime –
the bombing of Al-Ahli Baptist Hospital. Almost a thousand lives gone in one breath – children, patients, doctors. Did the pilot pause? Did he wonder: *This is a hospital… should I really bomb it?*

And then, the journalists. A tent, not a battlefield. Ahmad Mansour, burned alive while sitting on a chair. He couldn't even stand up to escape. The fire swallowed him – and the world watched.

Did the soldier know?
Did he care?
This was a journalist. *Why was he a target?*

And the infant – a baby who never opened his eyes to life, who died from hunger. Starvation. Did those who block food at the border stop to ask: *What was his crime?*

The pregnant woman, the nursing mother, who needs extra nutrition to support her baby – she collapses in the street because there's nothing to eat. Did they ask, even once: *What has she done to deserve this?*

The questions don't end.

But the one that echoes through every tent, every grave, every broken home, is:

When?

When will the world,
so proud of its humanity, wake up and see what is happening in Gaza?

When will the Arab nations rise
for their brothers and sisters – starving, slaughtered, displaced?

And when will this nightmare end –
this nightmare I pray, with all my heart,
is just a dream…
that will vanish when I wake up?

My cheek on my arm

Ahmed Raed Mohammed Farhan

This was once our refuge –

The sanctuary we fled to in sorrow,

The place where our thoughts would roam freely,

As we lifted our eyes to the sky, to the stars,

Or surrendered ourselves to the wonders of nature,

Letting emotions flow – joy, sadness, longing –

Or finding calm in the familiar features of someone we loved,

Drifting gently in a daydream, floating on clouds of soft cotton.

But now…

That once-elegant state of mind has shattered –

No longer a haven, but a ruin.

Now, it's filled with madness and debris,

Echoing with the cries of grieving mothers,

The sobs of children,

The wails of orphans.

I've lost the sense of beauty in the passing days.

The past has turned into painful images,

Spinning like a reel around my eyes –

Each frame a memory I wish I could escape.

I curl up, head pressed to knees,

Trying to hide from it all – but even then, it seeps in.

Even the call to prayer doesn't bring peace anymore –

Instead, it opens the gates to poisonous thoughts that attack the mind.

I no longer know where to flee.

Sometimes, I find myself thanking God

just for the presence of my hands… and my cheek.

Because I don't know –

Has someone out there lost the place where a hand meets a cheek?

Or has the cheek been lost…

Because the head itself has been torn away

Starvation in the era of modernity

Ahmed Raed Mohammed Farhan

It is said that the deepest physical weakness a human experiences comes at two stages in life:

The first is after birth – a weakness that is gently accepted by both society and self, wrapped in love and tenderness.

The second is in old age – a weakness beyond one's control, met with frustration from self and pity from others, shadowed by helplessness.

But here in Gaza, we know a third kind.
A kind that strikes the infant, the youth, the elderly, the child, and the adult – male and female alike.
It makes no distinction.

Its cause?
People stripped of humanity, who wield it as a weapon of war.
Yes – **starvation**.

Starvation seeps into us like cancer – slow, consuming, paralyzing.
It makes our shoes feel heavier as we walk,
our hands tremble as we lift a glass of water,
our backs curve as we try to stand,
our joints crack as we reach for toys – trying to forget this hunger.

But how can we forget, when our stomachs are hollow,
and their growls echo painfully through the silence?
When hunger's moan becomes a haunting melody in our ears,
reminding us of the cruelty we endure?

We see it in our ribs,
in the hollows of our arms and chests,
in the way belts no longer cling to shrinking waists.
We feel it even in sleep –
a nightmare gnawing at our dreams,
stealing the softness of slumber, replacing it with salt-filled tears
that my little one wipes from his cheek

before they soak into his pillow.

There is no escape –
not in dreams,
not in reality,
not in a world that should, by now, be at the height of compassion
    and progress.

Yet it strips itself bare,
revealing the lie of its civility –
powerless in the face of hunger,
the weapon of a state infected with the plague of fascism,
reigning unchallenged in tyranny,
as it has for 78 years.

Screaming

Obay Jouda

Today, after four months of screaming…. no one is here.
Four months of voices echoing into the void,
not a single ear caught their cry.

Four months of hunger...
we no longer remember what a loaf of bread looks like.
Everything here is edible except bread.

We feast on memories,
chew on the brittle skins of dry onions,
boil wild herbs and whisper to our stomachs:
"This is soup."

The children of the neighborhood
have memorized the names of animal feed.
They cheer if an apple peel falls
from the back of an ambulance.

I haven't tasted sugar in four months.
Even sugar has become a luxury.

For four months,
I've been counting time by the number of times
I stand at the doorway of the shattered mosque,
eyes fixed on the sky,
waiting for a miracle that never arrives.

And I scream, I say:
You are now in the greater cell.
A room of shattered stone and a ceiling that droops low –
but no real walls.

Because the greatest dungeon needs no walls.
It needs only a world that chooses not to see while it sees,
that chooses not to hear while it hears.

We live in a forest.
Not because there are trees,
but because there is no mercy.

No one hears you.
No one *wants* to hear you.
No one here hears the screaming
or perhaps, no one wants to hear it.

The scream of an empty stomach.
The wail of a mourning mother.
The howl of a city.
The roar of falling shells.
The crying of children.
The screaming of grown men.

There is no time here for anything except screaming.
No time for tomorrow.
No time for hope.
Not even time for an embrace.

Perhaps someone might save us
from a torment that hasn't slept in two years.

Since I opened my eyes to this world,
the wind has howled without pause.
I remember no comfort.
I remember no full day.

All I remember is the screaming.

The screams of the voiceless
who, this time, *"did knock on the walls of the tank"*
but it was never they who were silent…

It was those inside the room who were deaf.

Captivity and Loss... Two Wounds That Never Heal

Eslam Anwar Gondy

On the 7th of October 2023, we woke up to the sounds of rockets.
At first, we didn't understand what was happening, but after following
the news, we realized that the Palestinian resistance had launched an
operation against the occupation. We felt joy in the beginning, but
things quickly turned around, and the suffering of Gaza's people began.

My family and I live near the border, so we had to leave our home
immediately. We moved between several relatives' houses due to the
bombing and threats. At first, we took shelter in my grandfather's
house, then kept moving from one place to another. During this period,
my aunt Na'ma, her husband, and their children were martyred, a huge
tragedy for our family. My brother Ahmad was also injured twice, once
in Al-Ahli Baptist Hospital and the second time by a bullet that nearly
hit his heart.

We experienced long periods of extreme hunger. We were forced to eat
corn flour, animal feed, and toxic wild plants, it was all we could find,
as the occupation blocked goods and aid from entering Gaza. There
was no food to buy or eat. We lived in one room with other families
we didn't know. This made movement and eating very restricted; no
one had enough privacy or freedom like we used to have at home, and
problems were constant. We cooked using firewood and carried water
over very long distances, and it was never enough for daily use because
of its scarcity.

For a while, we lived in Al-Shifa Hospital, until one night the Israeli army surrounded it. They began forcing us out of the hospital in groups – first the men, then the women under extremely harsh conditions. They took my father, my brother, and other male family members with men from other families at night in heavy rain. They tortured them, letting some go and arresting others. My brother was among those arrested, as were some of my cousins. They stripped them of their clothes in the freezing cold and pouring rain, but they let my father go, forcing him to leave alone in the dark, stormy night.

My mother, sister, and I remained in the hospital, not knowing what had happened to my brother and father. The next day, the army called us to come down so they could evacuate us. We left and passed by tanks. My mother went first, but when I tried to follow, they told me not to and ordered us to go back into the hospital, promising to evacuate us the next day. They separated us. That night was one of the hardest in my life gunfire was everywhere, we heard prisoners being tortured, and we had nothing to sleep on. All we could think about was: what happened to our father and brother?

In the morning, they called us again, and we exited past tanks. I had never felt humiliation like that in my entire life. We barely made it out and reunited with my mother and father. My brother Ahmad had been arrested and suffered severe torture in Israeli prisons. We endured psychological torture as we didn't know whether he was alive or not. After two months of suffering, he was released on May 2, 2024, but they released him in the south while we were in the north, we remained separated.

Then came the greatest tragedy on June 21, 2024, when the municipality garage where my father worked was bombed. My father was martyred in the attack – an indescribable shock. My father was our only support, my beloved, a priceless treasure. Words can never express my feelings, but his martyrdom broke our backs. I was affected mentally and financially after his loss. We couldn't even visit his grave – the occupation bulldozed it.

We then moved between schools and destroyed buildings. Every time we thought we were safe, we were surprised by a new bombing or threat of invasion. We lost our home twice. Each time, we hoped to return to it, but the occupation deprived us even of this simple right.

Our living conditions became unbearable: not enough food, no water, no electricity, and no safety. My siblings were separated from us, Ahmad in the south, and my older brother Sobhi in Egypt. We could barely contact them due to the loss of internet and communication networks. And our father… he was martyred.

Every day, we live hoping this war will end. We've lost everything: our home, our father, our dreams, and our stability. The war destroyed every part of our lives – emotionally, physically, socially, and educationally. And now, we don't even know if we'll live to see the end, or if we'll be the next victims.

The loaf we die for

Raghad Ahed Alsafadi

We now live in a version of Squid Game stripped of fiction, no cameras, no drama, no prize money glittering at the end.

There, people sacrifice for millions.

Here, we risk our lives for a sack of flour that doesn't even satisfy our hunger, yet we depend on it completely.

In the game, death is scripted.

Here, death is routine, it walks through queues, lurks in empty kitchens, and echoes in the silent cries of mothers with nothing to feed their children.

A loaf has become a badge of valor.

A crumb, an act of survival.

And the mill turns, not only on grain, but on our bones, our silence, and our vocabulary of hunger.

How ironic… that bread, which sits untouched on plates around the world, offered as a casual side, often ignored,

has become here the backbone of survival.

To obtain it isn't ordinary… it's victory.

We are playing, not to win, but simply to exist for one more day.

And this reality…

is more savage than any fiction, and more merciless than any story ever written for a screen.

When Food Becomes a Dream

Farah Abomutayr

At 2 a.m., the Ramalawi family was awakened by the cries of their eight-year-old daughter, Mariam. She was sobbing and screaming from intense hunger. Her stomach hurt terribly, and she had lost seven kilograms in less than three months.

Before the war, Mariam was like a princess among girls – living her childhood in pure innocence, never having harmed anyone. She was like an angel.

Mariam fell asleep again, exhausted by pain, crying, and screaming. But her parents remained awake, sitting silently, thinking about their innocent little girl, worn down by hunger and fatigue.

Mariam had written in her diary:
"I don't know why we have no food. Have we become poor?"

She nudged her father, who was lost in thought beside her:
"Daddy, have we become poor?"

The father couldn't find an answer. He began asking himself...
Is a doctor who earns a thousand dollars a month considered poor?

He answered himself:
– Certainly not.

The problem is that prices in the market are sky-high, and there's barely anything available to buy. Withdrawing money from the bank carries huge fees – up to 40% of the amount. A thousand dollars, which used to be more than enough before the war, is now not enough at all.

A long and complicated answer, but he kept it to himself.

"No, my daughter, we haven't become poor. It's just that prices are very high these days. Maybe they'll go down soon – I hope so."

He thought he had escaped her question, but in truth, it stayed with him, echoing in his mind again and again.

Meanwhile, Mariam's mother was lighting a fire to cook lentils – the food that had become a staple for every family in Gaza: for breakfast, lunch, and dinner. Everyone's stomachs were worn out from eating lentils so often.

Mariam called out to her:
"Mom, Mom, what are we going to eat for lunch today?"
"Lentils, as usual, my dear."
"But I'm tired of eating lentils, Mom. I've lost so much weight, and my stomach hurts every day because of it."
"If only we had another option, my daughter. But we're forced to eat it. We have no other choice. Go to sleep now, and I'll wake you when the food is ready."
"Okay, Mom. But I'm really hungry. I hope I don't have to wait too long."

Mariam fell asleep, and the night passed, without food.

As for the meal her mother pretended to prepare, it was just a trick to help Mariam sleep.

They didn't even have lentils.

A Bag of Flour Worth Life and Blood

Farah Abomutayr

At 4 a.m., Ahmad and his father woke up after sleeping on the ground near the aid truck crossing point. They drank some water and sat waiting for the trucks to arrive. Two hours later, the trucks entered, and people rushed toward them with force and desperation. Some were trampled underfoot, others punched in the face. A few managed to reach the trucks and grab a bag of flour after immense struggle and pain.

At that moment, three Israeli tanks stood nearby, watching the starving crowd scramble for aid. Ahmad noticed one of the soldiers pointing toward the others and saying a few words.

Then Ahmad screamed:
"Run! Run quickly! Get down! They're going to shoot – get down!"

He realized the gestures and words he'd seen were a green light to open fire. Within seconds, the area turned into chaos – dust in the air, blood on the ground.

"Father! Father! Where are you, Dad?"

As the dust settled and people scattered, Ahmad searched frantically for his father, who had vanished at the first shot. Martyrs lay everywhere. The wounded screamed. The stench of blood and death filled the air.

"Dad! Can you hear me? Look at me! Please, Dad, look at me!"

Ahmad found him – his father, lifeless, soaked in blood and dirt.

"Dad… I wish we hadn't come. Please answer me. Look at me, Dad…"

They had run out of flour days ago. They wouldn't have come unless it was necessary. Who would walk willingly into death for a bag of flour?

Ahmad lifted his father and walked to the ambulance point. He placed him on a stretcher and took him to the morgue – so he could be washed and buried with dignity.

"Mom… Dad… Dad is gone. Dad was martyred, Mom… Dad was martyred!"

Ahmad collapsed, sobbing uncontrollably. After a long silence, he whispered:

"A bag of flour… worth a life and blood."

A Supplication to Revive the Future

Ahmed Raed Mohammed Farhan

From a dreamer with vision, eager to decorate life with a bright future in what they always called "the golden age of your twenties" to someone now buried beneath rubble, vision shattered, thoughts confined by catastrophe.

I was once full of life, driven by a hunger for knowledge, believing that success and learning were the only paths to prove my worth – my way to lead, to rise.

But overnight, my life collapsed into a vast, directionless void.
I don't know if I keep walking this tunnel, will light appear at the end?
Or will the darkness grow heavier, closing in from all sides,
like a monster that stormed into my world without knocking?

Yes, I'm still holding onto my dreams.
But the question that haunts me is:
Will I be alive in the next moment to fulfil them?
And if I survive this minute – will I survive the next hour?
The next day? The next year?

These questions of survival or death, hope or despair
have become my prison.
I can't find a way out.

Now, I live like a prisoner
a body barely functioning,
a soul collapsing.

And then another question:
What's the purpose of living
if all I have are fragments of hope,
fragments of dreams,
fragments of a soul?

This is exactly what the Zionist machine of terror continues to do
with every form of torture and madness.
And I, I feel madness closing in.

To you, a society that prides itself on culture and responsibility,
you know what it means to have your rights stripped away,
to feel your spirit break.

So I ask you:
If you are truly free
then help save a free voice
before I, too, become just another number

on the daily list of the mourning
a list that, tragically, has become
a way of life.

As for me...

POEMS

Winds of Resolve

Donya Mohammed Sameh

Here I am, living the very moment
Standing on the edge of the cliff

Unafraid of the inevitable
Nor the fog of the depths
I open my arms and welcome every wind
You find me falling, many times
Becoming a heap of blackness

I do not rest
I gather my failures and move forward
I do not tire of reinventing myself
Rising was a crossing toward what I should be

I savour the bitterness of pain
A heavy breath at every battle
How delicious was pain then
How agony refined me

Ashes and Ink

Donya Mohammed Sameh

A flame of passion beams
From the ashes of my burning soul
In writing, lies ecstasy
So much of it
Immersively, I never wrote

But now, I drown
In the whirlpool of emotion
Internal hunger compels me
To write what captivates me
To trace our days, our past

Like a cup of coffee
I savour its taste
Contemplating its flavour
As if for the very first time

Traceline of a boat
Yearning for every harbour
Longing to drop the anchor

I await the end of the road
And here we are
Counting days
Charting a course
Weaving a destination
And you will find me here
Immersed in prose
And literature

Fear Beneath Silence

Donya Mohammed Sameh

Endlessly, the mind wanders
To the periods of before
Nostalgia for the beauty of their moments
Realized my longing was
For the tranquillity of my mind
The peace of my soul
My comforted heart

There is silence everywhere
Except inside of me
Peace prevails
Not in my homeland
Serenity not knocking my door

I long to be comforted
By a slice of solace

Why this feeling pours inside
When peace breezes by
Drops of water from my face
Slide onto my ears

Soul wounds on me, tighten
As if peace tabooed in my land

Fear threads tighten
To suffocate my soul
Four letters planted a feeling
Gnawing at every wound.
Time heals wounds,
But don't you see
One feeling can last a lifetime!

I Wish I Were a Bird One Day

Linda Alhawari

I wish I were a bird one day
Flying without restrictions
Crossing countries and seas
No limits nor permits

No visa would I need, no entry stamp
No global humiliation just to pass a ramp

Nothing left for me here
No home, no dignity, no cheer

I see me aged years in a month
Let alone in 24 months and worse

The rubble of my home
Stares back at me,
The stones of my room whispering
Will we never meet again?
Is this our last glimpse, so I go in a mirage?

We built it with our eyes
Ornamented it with our hearts
I planted a tree
Watered with joys of my soul

I see you go before your time
Who will replace my memories, my dreams?
Do I have anyone but Allah
To hear my moans?

One Year of Genocide

Jood Sabea

A sun used to shine
Loved her golden yellow
Her warmth; my life
It was beaming
Even in the darkest days
She gave me warmth
Sent it down to me
In gentle rays
A shimmer of hope
Reassuring me
Light is coming again
As the sun usually does
She sets for a time
And returns brighter
With her same passion
Same kindness
With a smile that fades beneath its flash
My sun reminds me of smile in a miserable situation
Like a bandage on a wound
She continues her path
In a world known for opposites
Day and night
Up and down

My life was radiant
Total eclipse; my sun absent
A year almost of cold days
My night is long
And my sun is not here
As I bleed
Without a bandage
And a smile absent
I know
In the depths of my heart
Tomorrow the sun will rise
And I so much love the morning

When the Fading Began

Yasmeen Ramadan Mohammad Omar

They used to say that war has a deafening sound
But I heard nothing but silence
A heavy silence, preceding the explosion
Followed by unseen devastation, yet I felt it dwelling within me
Nothing in the war of the heroism they spoke of
I wasn't a soldier, I did not carry a weapon
But I was the target
I was the ground they trod on
The soul torn apart by terror in waves
Everything around me, turned into ashes
Inside me, everything crumbling
Like an old wall bombarded a thousand times
I don't tremble in the face of pain,
Nor do my features break in the face of traumas
I am used to staying solid when everyone trembles
I am used to staying silent when my inside screams
Despite all this steadiness, I am afraid
I am afraid of waking up to a tragedy
I am afraid of suddenly losing

The one I love,
To find the house empty
The voice absent
My memory filled with the unbearable
I do not fear war as much as I fear loss
War strikes the body
But loss slowly eats away the soul
Laving you alive, not to live but to reminisce
I hide this fear behind fixed eyes
Behind features that reveal nothing,
But my heart
My heart trembles with every second time passes
I do not know who will stay
Who might leave without saying goodbye
Do you know what it means to fall asleep every night
    whispering the name of those you love
As if you are saying goodbye to them without even noticing
Do you know what it means
To wish for death not because you are weak
But you cannot bear the thought of being alone without them
My heart began to fade the day I realized that nothing lasts
That faces I see every day could be a memory tomorrow
The fading began when I began counting the names in my mind
Imagining who might be taken first
I don't cry, I don't collapse
But place my hand on my heart every time I hear an explosion
Counting the numbers, counting my breaths
And begging God: "Don't make this day my worst day"
Every beat in my chest is loaded with anticipation
Every laugh I share with them I save
As if I fear it won't happen again
I no longer live life as I used to
I live on the edges of fear
On the fringes of prayer
I try to appear as I used to,
But something inside me fades every day
I fear that one day
I turn into a rigid skeleton
With no longing, no tears, no life

And here I am
Resisting to collapse
But I know for certain that I don't fear war
Rather, I fear war will leave me without loved ones

A War on Fragile Hearts That Wanted to Live – Only to Die a Thousand Times

Tasneem Ramadan Mohammad Omar

Loss, or rather, losing someone you love, is forever painful, isn't it? Well, this pain, the nature of which I never understood, I have felt and learned in the most severe way. Sar mercilessly robbed me of my loved ones.

Yes, I lost my soul in this war, and I now have nothing, but broken fragments live inside of me. Loss cannot be described in words, but I can say that it is like your soul leaving your body without dying and your heart dead without being stabbed or pulse stopped. This pain is much greater to be described in just lines or in a few words.

You will lose the sense of yourself, your body, or even what is happening around you because the pain in your heart exhausts you. You try to move forward, but you remember that they are no longer around you. They will not rejoice in your joy or grieve in your sadness. They will not be there when you need them.

I was like an impregnable dam, facing life with a bright unfading smile but the loss of my refuge and safehaven destroyed my fortresses and turned them into rubble. The pain has consumed me, but I am still breathing. Yes, I am alive, but I got no feeling. They killed my heart and took away my soul. They made her lie under dirt, a cold body. I hear her voice everywhere; I see her picture on every wall and in every face. They made me lose my innocent angel and left me to walk the path we drew together alone, without refuge or guide. They left me alone without my impregnable fortress to face the ugliness of life. And if they stop this war, who will restore my heart and my refuge? Who will restore the souls that were dear to my heart? Who will silence the nostalgia and memories that flow in my mind? Who will compensate me for the warmth of the hearts I lost? Who will calm this deadly pain that runs through my heart and soul? No one, no one will ever do.

I feel lost and confused without my angel and my beloved friend, my soulmate. So, will you bring her back to me so she can guide me again? I have no one but her who understands me without explaining. Will you bring my angel back to me? Will you bring back my companion who you stole with your missiles? Will you bring her back so we can continue walking together towards the dream we share? Will you do this?

I cannot stand it any more!! I am dying slowly here. Yes, I do laugh and tell everyone that I am fine, but I am not. My soul is shattered and scattered. Would you kindly rearrange and reassemble it as I cannot bear all of this. I am still in the prime of my youth, so why all this pain? Why all this loss? Why am I not fine? Why am I dying slowly? Why should I lose myself before I even find it? Why do I have to suffer all this, I am only human, with dreams and ambitions. A human who had friends planned to achieve dreams with. Why were my friends taken away from me so brutally? Why am I lost alone without them around me? Why is fate so cruel? Will this situation and this war ever end, or will I vanish before I find myself? If only it would stop without me losing more. My strength has failed. I am no longer able to bear more loss. My energy has run out and my tears have all dried up. So, be gentle with a heart that has only just become familiar with life, or will the world remain deaf and not hear my voice?

Written by a heart tormented by excessive pain.

I Write from the Heart of War, Not Its End

Raghad Ahed Alsafadi

I write knowing with absolute certainty that I am no longer the same –
 and never will be again.

Everything in me has changed, shattered, and shifted.

Memory is no longer a shelter, nor is the soul capable of preserving
 its former self.

War devoured us from within – not suddenly, but dead slow

The first nights of displacement carved deep in my memory
Threats against our neighbourhood

We ran into the streets
Carrying children in one arm and terror in the other

We moved from one house to another – not because we were
 turned away
Because every house we enter, we are soon told: "It's no longer safe"
We flee again, clutching our trembling bodies in our light pyjamas
Searching for the shadow of a wall to shield us from a shell
 anytime it appears

That night, we slept in the courtyard of a hospital
We sat on the bare ground watching death hover above our heads
When dawn rose in the dark
We went home surrendering ourselves to blind fate
Murmuring the *shahada* prayer in case we die on our way
Whispering it into our chests as if bidding the world goodbye
 on the tiptoe of death
The next day, our neighbour killed

He had stayed with us just last night
They bombed his home entirely
Since then, the sound of drones has never left me
It clings to my breath

Has now become part of the distorted familiarity we live in
We fear their silence more than their noise
The thud of anything hitting the ground makes our hearts leap
Thinking another missile knocking on the edge of the end

I longed for my bedroom that embraced me

For a bed whose folds I know
For a door, its creak I recognize
For a bathroom I do not have to beg for a turn
For a moment of comfort – untimed, unwarned, unpanicked

I long for the comfort I once enjoyed
Not knowing I possessed a fortune that didn't last.
I write now from a tent that has become my home
My own house has been destroyed.
I sleep on the ground, exhaustion is my pillow
Trying to be okay even though everything around me is collapsing

We were displaced fourteen times or more
Each time, I carried my father's picture
Except for the last time
I left in a hurry, leaving it behind
How I wished I could go back and get it
I felt I lost him again for the second time

Sometimes I say to myself: Perhaps it would have been more merciful
for the picture to stay there, to rest from displacement

Perhaps it would have been kinder for my father not to be here
in this devastation

If he was alive, he would have been consumed by running in search
of shelter, and would have died a thousand times trying to bring
us food

Worry would have consumed him, just as it had consumed his friend
Who disappeared for days to be found lying in a hole killed
Along with those with accompanied him
They had only gone to bring food

Can you imagine a person being killed simply because
he wanted to feed his children?

To be buried in silence while his family keeps searching for him
among graves

My niece of eight years once said to me:
"Even if I ate all the bread in the world,
Nothing would erase the taste of the fodder you ground instead of flour
That taste will never leave my mouth
It will remain a witness to the hunger that consumed our souls."
She told me about the soldier at the checkpoint,
He separated her from her mother
How he pointed his rifle at her childish face as if threateningly.
She asked me: "Was I scaring him?
Did he imagine that, at the age of eight, I intend to blow myself up?
I was the terrified one
But his rifle was trembling before me."

I wish for a simple life, not a luxurious one
To only live without terror
Without long queues for water
Without screaming for shelter
But today
I cry from hunger
I break down from helplessness
I shatter when I can't find a decent place of dignity
To use as a restroom

When I look at my mother's wrinkled face
I am overwhelmed with grief
She could have rested after my father has gone
To see her granddaughters grow before her
But today she sits by the dusty tent
Struggling in silence

Every home in Gaza
Has a story of loss, a wall of pain

My aunt; was a mother and a friend to me
Was displaced with us, suffered with us, then departed,
I write about her as if she were still here

Jumana... that little girl I saw
A future mother
Was killed with her parents
In a massacre at the market

My father's friend, the kind pharmacist
Was killed inspecting his pharmacy reduced to rubble

My neighbour, the university professor
Told me one day, "This place is no longer safe,"
And then passed away

My friend
Her laughter was a breeze
Today... there is no breeze

Can you imagine a day when you'll have to fight for a sip of water?
To cry from hunger?
To collapse as you cannot find a place of dignity to freshen up
To pray for death, not because you hate life
Because you are tired of enduring it

I ask myself over and over again:
What did we do to deserve all this?

Every day we live here – a year of pain
Every moment – a new chapter of loss

I miss myself
I miss my niece, whom I know I'll never love anyone like
I miss who we were before this insanity, before this slow collapse

And I ponder, until when?
Will we ever emerge from this rubble?
Or will our voices be forever buried?

And the dream continues
And the story continues

White Banner

Lina Khattab

Blood soaked the white banner,
Peace scattered in vain
The doves took flight
Only death waved in the streets

Words fell silent
Tears turned into stone
We stood gathering children's dreams
But they perished
Only toys remained

We bid farewell at every threshold
Entrusted wills and wishes to the wind
Left so much behind,
Stumbled on, groping for dawn

A dawn to make us forget
The bullet's sting, the shell's betrayal
In the old house, laughter faded
Jasmine withered
Grief loomed over balconies like shadow

We walked on, weighed down by strangers' stares
The stamp of exhaustion etched in memory
The streets swelled – it was Judgment Day
Who reshaped the city?

Where are the mosques?
Who shattered the churches?
Who burned the schoolbooks?
Who put out the city's light, its joy?

We stayed alone, battling time.
Our blood seeped through the cursed streets
Through the plundered homeland
Explosions bloomed as ceasefires were vetoed

Here, life is cheap
Nothing stirred
Hunger and cold gnawed
At the limbs of the sleeping
While the world looked on

Nightmare on Gaza

Hazem

In this soul-exhausting, nerve-wracking, and hope-shattering war,
grief and sadness have come smiling mockingly at the people of Gaza.
Bringing with them all shades of pain and suffering.

How many mothers have lost their children? How much money has
been wasted? How many fathers have their children called martyrs?
How many homes have been destroyed? How many lives have been
broken? How many smiles have been burned and disfigured?

How many have been left homeless? How many children have been
orphaned?

This is not a war, but a nightmare descended upon us from which we
are still unable to wake up.

The Closed Window

Marah Alaa El-Hatoum

I passed by many windows during my displacement. Most were open
with iron bars and mesh, which were useless for keeping out flies
and mosquitoes, especially at night. Sometimes those bars shared
drawings of leaves, or curved iron in the shape of two heart-shaped
objects. One of them was at eye level, and another was high up, not
for looking through, but for bringing in air to keep me alive. We would

close it with a black plastic bag in the cold. One of them overlooked the clotheslines, and behind them was a small clementine tree whose fruit had dried up, no longer edible for humans or even insects, for that matter. I never saw a bee landing on the tree with its wings, seeking food but it was a beautiful sight nonetheless; something that still bore its colour even though it was very dead.

I am not truly alive

Marah Alaa El-Hatoum

I am not truly alive

I still breathe, and I feel my heart pounding with panic
I flee and escape, carrying my limbs intact
I have my family, my senses
These are blessings, yes
But constantly under threat
They are all I have
I am not listed among the dead, nor the missing, nor even the living
I live as though I am a passing shadow
Owned by no one, unworthy of a life
I live with one hope: that someday
I might truly live
That we all might live
A blessing we've neither seen nor felt
Sometimes I wonder – is life a blessing, a miracle,
Or merely a distant goal, forever outside my reach?
I do not know the difference between
Nearing death and beginning life
I know both are too narrow
For one to embrace me
And if within me lives an impossible wish
It is the wish to live

The children have changed

Marah Alaa El-Hatoum

The children have changed,

but they still carry something we adults have lost:
not innocence but the very identity of childhood.
Even that, though, suffers like us from hunger, fear, poverty, disease.
Even childhood is killed here.
Our children grow up believing that war is life.
They long for apples as if they were impossible miracles once within
    their reach, now a dream. They cry when the bread runs out
    because to them, bread is the lifeline of existence.

Life teaches them nothing but this:
someone is trying to kill you.
So run. Escape. Panic.
If you want to survive.

Crying, screaming – this has become their language.
    Hunger, fear, and exhaustion this is their routine.
We fear they'll one day meet children not in war –
    and realize the difference.
If we told them what their lives were like before the war,
they would understand the gap – between life… and war.

I know a child who became an orphan
before he was even born – before his mother knew he was a boy,
not a girl.

When night falls

Marah Alaa El-Hatoum

When night falls,

we go to sleep while being half-hungry, one-quarter alive, and the
remaining quarter longing to sink into a deep, endless slumber.

But then, that cruel insomnia strikes –

forcing you to review your day, recall your past, and contemplate a
    future that offers no guarantees.

You hold on to hope.
Perhaps, one day, a bold dream will come true –
a dream that defies war and siege,
a dream that is not nourished by food, but by sheer will.

Words arrive in strange, fleeting images –
followed by tears,
reminding them of this bitter reality.

Dreams begin to wither.
Imagination collapses, sick and exhausted, on the ground.
There's no bed for a human being in war –
    not in reality, not even in dreams.

Tears pour down
like your throat yearns for water one day.
Thunder roars inside the mind,
floods of tears surge –
yet silence always stays close.

Everyone is trapped in a kind of sleep
that doesn't protect them from war.
Each person lives out their fears within that sleep,
dreading to wake up and find one of those fears has become real –
or worse, fearing they may never wake up again,
and so hope would die with them.

No one truly finds rest,
even in slumber.

Suddenly –
a bloody noise,
violent tremors shake the earth,
stones fall from the ceiling,
cutting through my silence and their sleep alike.

The innocent children, raised to believe that war is life,
were terrified.
They screamed, cried, panicked –
then fell back asleep,
joining the adults in the traps of this sleep.

My mind no longer wants to think.
My eyes have stopped crying.
My body is limp.
I must join the sleep.

I shift my position,
trying to find comfort on the floor.
I close my eyes to the sound of the dawn call to prayer: God is great.

A letter to the dead

Marah Alaa El-Hatoum

I don't know who I'm speaking to.
I don't know who to send this letter to.
What should I say?
All I know is this: I hope you're okay.
And I hope no one else finds the path you took and follows it.
My condolences to those you left behind –
the broken pieces of loved ones who tried to convince death they
wanted to join you.
To the children who still carry you in memory,
never knowing your legacy,
only that you were once here.
Will words about you live on,
or will they die, like everything else around us?

Or maybe, they'll be born again every time we feel we're dying –
and your memory will come to us,
beautifying this grim reality.

Oh Allah, the Creator of me and of him,
ease our pain, forgive us,
and grant us eternal paradise –
not this short life.
And let us end our lives with a happy ending.

The Tragedy of a Palestinian Student

Laila Lubbad

It was the darkest day of my life.

That morning, full of hope and energy, I was preparing to head to my university on the seventh of October – exactly at 6:30 a.m. – when everything collapsed.

In a single moment, life turned upside down.

My dreams, my ambitions, all the paths I had carved out with years of struggle, crumbled into dust.

I had spent years battling illness, hoping to travel for treatment and break free from the grip of poverty.

But in a heartbeat, everything vanished – my home, my memories, my childhood, my achievements – all reduced to ash.

Since that terrible morning, not a single hour has passed without my mind drowning in questions about a future I can no longer see.

Will I ever be whole again?

Will my body heal?

Will I ever breathe without this crushing weight on my chest?

Will this war end without leaving me with yet another scar – another tragedy to carry?

Will I see my family smile like before?

Will I walk the halls of my university once more?

Will I continue my education, or has that dream, too, been stolen?

Will I...?

And will I...?

Endless questions echo in my mind, and none have answers.

I cling to the hope that this war will end.

I dream of a day when my thoughts are not consumed by trauma, when my body is not riddled with pain, when sitting, or even sleeping, is not a burden.

There is so much I want to say, yet words fail to capture the full depth of what I've lived through.

No string of sentences can truly convey the ache in my soul, the silence of my destroyed home, the scream buried in every memory.

All I wish – so simply, so quietly – is that my dreams might one day bloom again.

That this violence, this endless war, this brutal erasure of lives and hopes, will finally stop.

Even if my dreams were humble, they were mine.

And they deserved to live.

From the heart of the deluge

Ruba Saqer

Racing heartbeats and a tempest of tangled thoughts.

I catch my breath and wonder:
Is this the end?

Perhaps "no," still echoed deep within me
perhaps the warmth of family stirred a flicker of calm within me.
But it was the end –
the end of innocence,
the death of youthful dreams buried before they ever saw light.

I never imagined it would end with me fleeing,
        running through the rubble
that smothers my chest and my hunger gnawing at my intestines.

I left behind the things I loved – my home!
Eyes anchored to the past,
arms wrapped around my fear,
while a reel of memories plays across my mind like tear-laden clouds:
a child's laughter chasing butterflies down the alley,
the old woman whispering prayers for every soul,
and you, oh dreamful girl – where are you going now?

Since that day, I remain displaced,
wandering and wondering
Where to?
Not just where to , but for how long ?
for how long will my people remain hungry, sick,
        and struggling to survive ?
Their eyes hold no shelter for life,
they overflow with longing for stolen spirits
and years swept away like dust.

their gaze shines with confusion silently asking ...
What happened here?
It is bruised with loss, fractured with grief,
but carries a shard of hope.

We see it shimmering on the horizon, rising through tongues of smoke.
We greet it – but never embrace it.
Still, it remains the beating heart of my people.

I write these words in the midst of ruin.
My ink runs red, mingled with blood.
Children's screams echo in my ears.
The blood still flows.

And so I write –
not to mourn,
but in hope that my words may be the ones to survive the deluge

Gaza is under the weight of war

Farah Akram Nofal

Here we are at a turning point in life
Here we are on the cusp of death and farewell
Here we are, amidst the cries of the martyr's mother
Here we are, amidst the weeping of the bereaved
    and the wailing of the infant
Who will provide formula for an infant that just got orphaned?
Who will come to comfort the longing of the widow
    and the martyr's mother?
Here we are, one step away from departing from our loved ones.
Who will become a martyr today, and who an orphan?
A moment of silence and reflection.
Who has pushed us into this abyss?
Who is to blame for the flowing blood?

Displacement and Fate

Farah Akram Nofal

Unleash your soul and let it sing
Let the ships anchor at their moorings
No one gets anything except what is destined for him
There are still ingredients that no one would have liked
We were angry about things that did not satisfy us
The winds blew and the days returned to give us patience
We were satisfied, but our satisfaction was not taken into account
After discontent comes what is not on our minds
The days will come back to us …
We say, "Oh, I wish we were satisfied with the destiny of our God "

Twenty in the Time of War

Heba Abuhussein

Tomorrow, I turn twenty – two decades inscribed with courage,
But it's not the courage that's sung
Rather, the courage that bleeds, endures, and survives

No cake can sweeten the smoke-filled air
No candles brighter than the flares
That stole my sky, burned my books
And turned my dreams to ash and dust

I should be in lecture halls
With pens and plans and quiet laughter
But I wear scrubs in shattered halls
My hand still trembling from the past

I stitched a wound when hope had gone
And hugged my brother as he wept
This is not how youth should be
But still, I am standing, I am alive

▲ Heba Abuhussein

I am not broken – I am flame
From the rubble of Gaza, I have become
A voice for those who cannot speak
And a heart, once again, that dares to dream

To My Dreams

Heba Abuhussein

To my dreams
On the other bank of the river
I am like an hourglass, my grains slipping

Each time I reach across to touch the other side
The rippling waters swallow up my elbows – like a jar sealed tight
Its stopper stubborn in the neck

On the first bank – where watermelon is a symbol – Gaza
Wandering in the whispers of the firewood
My head radiates with the glow of accomplished goals,
    consumed by the flames of war
Everything around me is silent
Except the cursed cell
In which the sounds echo; one after another
Every buzzing therein; a dream steaming in my head

Those moments drowned me in tears
Like a willow bowing to the ground
Not in prayer but in sorrow too heavy to bear
My passion never faltered
Even when the rusty lock – occupation – tries to suffocate it

I crawl, I strive slowly , nside the watermelon – Gaza, to no avail
The closer I get to my dream
Its features change and flees
As if testing my patience and faith

Days pass
But the dream is never completely dispersed

They tell me: Dream!
But I was born in a land where dreams die of hunger

My waist bones stick out, sharp as a gun sticking out of a rusty lock –
    the occupation.
Not from hunger but from that watermelon; Gaza
Where dreams die starving, too

Still,
A part of me still lives, somehow alive
Though the rusty lock, in all its cunning
May try to block my path
I shall go on dreaming
For there is still room to dream

To reach to most intricate – the tiniest details
I will reach the zenith –with my dreams

Living the Unwatchable

Farah Jeakhadib

Imagine yourself watching films about war – destruction everywhere, deep sorrow, killing everyone whether they are innocent or civilians, and famine while you just sit there watching, whether in pain or even amazed.

That is how it was for me before I witnessed this genocide myself. A genocide that stole our souls and dreams, leaving us bodies without souls. No – it stole our bodies too.

Now, when I watch films, I feel nothing. It is as if I have been stripped of emotions. A sarcastic smile creeps across my face as I automatically find myself saying: ''This isn't real.''

What we have been facing; s real. The killing and death that have become part of our daily routine; that is reality. The bombing that does not distinguish between the so-called "safe" places and others – that is reality. The hunger we have been suffering; that is reality.

The truth is happening in plain sight of the entire world, and all the world does is watch what should never be watchable on any screen. And the most painful part?

They have gotten used to it.

The Dream of Survival in a Merciless World

Sara Aaed Abass Alkhaldy

I don't know where my old features have gone, or how I can return to
   them.
A heavy, gloomy string of days descended upon us without warning.
They extinguished our spirits in every sense of the word.
They erased our expressions and replaced them with tearful eyes,
   hollow faces,
and turned us into people stripped of dreams, ambition, and passion.

They left us with only one wish: to survive.
And now, even that wish is on the verge of being stolen.
How vile this world is.
A silent world, entertained by watching people trapped in a place
they don't even have the option to leave –
sometimes burned alive, sometimes torn to pieces,
and other times simply starved to death.
A world so shameful, you feel embarrassed to be part of it.
Do you know what it feels like
for someone who once believed their best days had just begun,
who thought it was finally time to chase their dreams,
who had started building the version of success they've carried
        in their mind since childhood –
only to wake up to a catastrophe that reduced everything to ash
and took away everyone and everything they loved?
Now, that person is just trying to survive a new life –
one without a home, without belongings, without memories,
without their favorite food, or even enough food to get through the day.
A life that is purely primitive, stripped of the bare minimums of
        human existence.
It's a feeling close to pity – pity for yourself,
because you are nothing.
You feel invisible.
You are below zero.
I don't know how we're supposed to rise from this tragedy.
I don't know how a person who once dreamed of so much
can now only wish for their home,
and for an ordinary day from the past,
to heal from this hell.
I honestly don't know.

Our Freedom

Reem Alaa Khalel Al-Astal

It could not be for more than just one second, seeing nothing but darkness, hearing nothing but bombing sounds filled with fears, waiting for the moment you faint or the delusion you made yourself believe, holding each other's shaky hands, praying that the final moment be easier than the rest.

Here in the middle of nothing standing to face your moment after they faced theirs, not knowing how your death will look like. Or when will it come.

Running, powerless, waiting for a crime to be committed and a miracle to be made,

Everything is done, and nothing has changed, expressing the dehumanizing force that we are facing, not knowing what or who is next after all that has been done.

Looking for humanity to call out but it has disappeared a long time ago, either you die or end-up living as dead. Either you starve to death, or live staving in a moment away from death.

Losing our lives, families, friends, and homes because of nothing but because we come from this place and land.

Is living an ordinary life only for people who are superior to us? Why do we only have the harshest form of living? Were suffering and struggling made just for us?

Is all of that suffering because we stem from Gaza?

Because you are from Gaza, you witness a life of torture, famine, displacement, humiliation and a much more. You can never forget seeing people fleeing, looking for the bodies of their sons and daughters, the crash of that large building with a horror sound, the smell of the city filled with smoke, ashes and corpses or the street filled with blazed cars and bodies burnt to their bones.

One can never forget the dismembered legs; arms scattered all around or forcibly moving under the force of fire, the face of your innocent child killed and that arm left from your other child.

I cannot forget that widow that went looking for food for her children or that father who went fetching his son without knowing he was killed and will never return.

What is even more painful is to realize that all your hard work and savings to obtain get the place you called home has evaporated and al you are left with is nothing.

How about the first moment you learn about the loss of your family members; one after the other. I still cannot fathom this but there is no way to deny what we are confronting.

Read this and believe it or not:

Our freedom was born from occupation,

Our freedom was made from blood and tears,

Our freedom formed from a painful past no one believes

Our freedom made of decades of struggling to be free,

Our freedom made of an unforgettable past, a suffering present, and an unknown future.

Is there anything else left to be done?

Gaza – I Am Peace's Call

Ola Abdullah Suleiman Sheikh Al-Eid

I am the spirit rising where hope blooms
I build new bridges through the fading night
I carry dreams like birds prepared to fly
I am the heart of Gaza, great and imperishable

My name is the child who reaches out for dawn
My name is the mother whose love carries on
I am the whisper in the stillness of night
I am the breath that stirs a never-fading coming light

I hold in my hands courage and grace
I withstand storms, embrace each moment
I am home for dreams to soar
I am the strength that shines even the dark

I am the longing for peace deep within
I am the hope that unites us all
I shake the olive branches with great love
And call upon the people of the world: "Rise, to indulge in grace!"

I make the rain fall like blessings from sky
From the ashes rises a new pure light
I am the dove soaring calm and clear
The silent tear of a world sincere and honest

From the past, I build a palace of peace
I bind threads, so all conflicts cease
I send my voice beyond the vast horizon
To heal earth where dreams reside

I make the rivers sing; mountains listen
Distance fades among tender hearts
I am the hope that knows no end
I am Gaza – where peace grows life

Gaza – I Am the Hope Unbroken

Ola Abdullah Suleiman Sheikh Al-Eid

I am the voice in the heart of stillness

A fire that lights the smoke of madness
I am the child with tear-stained face
Still dreaming of a safer place

From rubble I build paths of life
I grow hope on crumbling edges
If hunger walks in where I remain
My spirit rises free from chain

I am the hope that calls out
The choking voice of a mother
Let aid flow in – not bombs and blight
Let books, not fire, fill the night.

Let olive branches heal the land
Not iron fists nor tightened hand
Unblock the gates, unseal the shore
Let lifelines reach to every door

I am the lantern when light dims
The ode of justice turns
Let mercy rain on tents and sand
To peace, bring the world to understand

I am the hunger, I am the call
The standing who will not fall
Let food and peace replace the fight
I am Gaza, I am what's right

Under the Sky with No Mercy

Samah Mustafa Youssef Bashir

Under a merciless sky, we stand
Not as shadows
But as flames engraved
On the wailing sand

The world rapidly passes us by
A thousand eyes
Not one sees
But we write our names in smoke

In queues for bread
In sung lullabies
Beside shattered balconies

They think we are silence
Contemplate we are dust
But our breath still rebels
In each whispered "why?"
Every funeral prayer
Rising like a banner
Above the rubble

Even the moon shies away
Afraid to see what has become
Of the children of salt and sun

But we do not break
We carry our deceased in our voices
Not for mourning
But for memories
We carry the city in our hearts
Its stones and songs
And stubborn light
That refuses to die

One day will come, when the smoke clears
Among us, justice dares to walk barefoot
You will find poems blossoming
From the cracks in our bones
Not written in ink but in life
That refused to be erased

The Voice of Gaza

Rawan Marwan Omar Matar

In Gaza lived a little boy
Dreaming of joy and great peace
He laughs, plays, and suns so free
Beneath the sun, near the sea

But darkness came without a sign
And stole his bright and hopeful time
No school, no songs, no games to play
Just fear and pain filled each day

His home destroyed, his heart now torn
No more laughter like times before
The world stays silent, yet he cries
As bombs still fall from burning skies

This is no tale of war alone
But children's grief, deep to the bone
So hear his voice, a pleading call
For hope to rise and peace for all

The Whirlpool of Grief and the Hope of Survival

Nour Mohammed Abusultan

A longing so deep
A sorrow so heavy
A suffocating breath
A setting sun
Days of life slipping away
Questions unanswered
Crying with no tears
Restless mind struggling within
The same question echoes again and again
Until when?

A whirlpool of thoughts keeps drowning me
Drowning me down deep
I try my all to survive
I pray to my Lord
Tears overflow
Heart is breaking
Unwavering hope in Him
I entrust to You, my Lord
All the locked doors and paths
For their keys are in Thy hands
And all tough matters
Easing them is simple for You

I went to Bed to Sleep

Nour Mohammed Abusultan

My day has come to an end.
I try to sleep, but
As usual, insomnia grips me tightly.
Countless reels spin in my mind…
The reel of today's events
Moments, words, expressions.
I blame myself for what I did,
Or maybe… I thank myself
For surviving yet another dull, draining day.
I try to think of a new routine,
Something anything
To bring even a spark of life
Into my lifeless days.
I try to recall what once made me happy,
And then a new reel begins
The reel of memories.
The one that used to lift me
In the darkest of days.
But now…

The moment that once made me smile
Brings me to tears.
I rush to stop my tears in two ways:
Either
I belittle the reason for my sadness
By comparing my sorrow to that of others:
"There are people who lost their families,
And here you are crying over a memory."
I remind myself:
Those I made those memories with
Are still alive by the grace of God.
There's still time to make more…
Even better ones.
Or
I remind myself that I am strong
A fighter,
Someone who faces pain and doesn't fall.
And so… the thoughts crash,
The memories collide,
A deep, heavy whirlpool
That saddens me,
Exhausts me.
Sleep finally wins.
I just hope I wake up
To a better reality.

The Grayness of Existence

Nour Mohammed Abusultan

I feel as if I am stuck in the middle
Between voidness and existence,
Between dark and light
Between chaos and silence
In the depths of a dimmed path
Leading nowhere
Neither to life so I rejoice in
Nor to death so I find rest

I am a fine thread hanging
Between presence and absence
I detest being trapped in this grey void
Not white enough to cheer my heart
Nor black enough to depress it
Just grey

As if my existence
Is merely an echo
Of an unspoken voice
An unborn shadow of a thing
Neither to spring so I blossom
Nor to autumn to fall
I swing between everything
Like a stranger forgotten by fate
between closed doors

As if I am in a blackhole
Empty space swallows me
Into infinite bottomless depths
Inside of me, everything overflows with chaos
Like an entire city in my heart
Whose walls crumpled

In my face doors shut whenever I near
Dreams fade whenever I approach

A hurricane of questions, doubt, and hesitation
With every step I take
I feel as if I am stepping onto a new illusion
Everything inside me is in turmoil
The grand question remains: "For how long?"

We live a lifeless life
A flowerless spring
A rainless winter
A summer whose sun
Burned away existence and dreams
An autumn where I see
Leaves falling and dreams perish

The Forgotten City

Waad Hamdi Allaham

We deserve life
Stop the fire, the destruction
Save the wounded
Alleviate the pain
Bury the dead and the darkness
Let the children eat bread and beans
Rise up for justice
Don't leave us alone
Let us see hope, let us see life
Why are you mute?
Are you pleased with the genocide?
We dream of peace
We are not fine
We are being killed all the time
We are under budlings rubble, under the sun and under the tents
Can you hear our voices?
We come from a living city that dreams of life

An olive tree above a forgotten grave

Sohair Rafat Hamdan

My name is Sohair
But they call me Hala
I am twenty autumns old
My petals fell a long time ago
My life is brief

I was weaned on my very first day
Crawled over thresholds soaked in blood
I love life
Yet life killed me time and time again
I love life
But live only its bitterness

I am the one who cries through the night
Lays her sorrow bare through the day

For a forgotten grave
Above which an olive tree planted
For a lost bird
That passed me by chance
Its eyes filled with tears

And still, I walk
I walk along the sidewalks of life
Passersby tell me: "Step down, walk over the crossing lines."
I approach them then pull back.

I, unlike others, gaze at them. My eyes fixed upon them
They are crossing lines – white!
So brilliantly white
But I am Palestinian
I fear that if I step forward
My feet will be severed

We die in it

Sohair Rafat Hamdan

I stare at the ceiling of the room

While in the background, missiles explode around the house

My home is just like a prison- – just a larger cell

Have you ever seen prisoners are in love with the ground of their cell?

We are entranced by it and killed for loving it

We quite literally die over it!

Speak, Journalize. Document. Capture – with no shame

Hada Mohammed Homaid

Speak of ruined homes, the rubble of stories
Journal the man burning in fire, the embodiment of the world's
    worse annihilation
Document the crowds of innocent people waiting desperately for food
    because that has become their greatest need
Capture videos for viewers to witness starvation, genocide, and famine.

Yes, the world watches – but no one moves, no one even feels
Were you every hungry, but had no food?
They are not asking for feasts – just a poor piece of bread
What about children crying because their stomachs are shrinking
    to starvation
Newborns dying to shortage of food, whose only sin
    is being born into the world's largest grave

This grave is built by the oppressor, the occupier, right in front of
    millions claiming to defend human rights and democracy.
Meanwhile, the people of Gaza are repressed and suffocated.
    Their greatest hope is to feel some connection to what is called
    "human life."
They want to sleep safely
To study in academic institutions.
To find something – anything – to eat.

Every morning, they walk in search of the bare minimum of human life
Water to drink, or water to clean but
Not in their homes but in fragile tents or should I say their sauna rooms
    in the blazing summer heat under chemical explosions.
Gaza's streets are filled with despair, exhausted by this life.
And today, even the nobles are going hungry.

Gaza's nobles are not hungry, they are being starved.

But they shall never be hungry in spirit. Their humility and dignity,
keeps them full even when their stomachs are empty. Their dignity is
bound to this land. Their humility is life itself, is life itself.
[sounds of explosions]

Gaza... The City That Does Not Break

Nadeen Shadi Ahmed

Gaza is not just a city; it is a tale of patience and resilience.
For many years, it lived under siege, enduring bombing and hunger,
    yet it refused to die.

In its streets among the rubble, life is born
Children go to school despite the fear
Mothers bake bread over fires amidst ruins
Young people plant hope in every corner

Every house in Gaza holds the story of a martyr
Every mother carries pain, yet raises her head and says:
"My son is a hero; he died for our dignity."

Despite the bombing, the call to prayer is raised
Prayers are held and flag is lifted
Gaza does not complain but speaks to the world:
"We are not just victims; we have rights, and we will neither leave
    nor be defeated"

In Gaza, everything speaks of life
Patience on the faces of people
Strength in the eyes of children
Dignity in the voice of each Palestinian that says:
"We shall return, no matter how long the oppression lasts."

Venus Fly Traps

Heba Abuhussein

In a land once heaped with wheat fields and olive trees
Where markets spilled lentils, flour and morning bread
We now walk beside dust. No wheat. No trees
Not even a whisper of olive oil or salt
The markets echo with nothing but emptiness

Hunger is not a hollow stomach – It's a Venus fly trap, sweet scented,
   red mouthed and waiting us as flies
It feeds on our skin,
Bites our muscles,
Chews our thoughts
Until we forget how to reflect.

My stomach folds in on itself
A silent cave echoing with groans
As ghrelin, weary from begging
Sends its final prayers to the brain
No answers, only silence

Hydrochloric acid
Once a soldier for digestion,
Now spills with no war to fight
Burning through the emptiness
As if my belly had turned on itself
In quiet revolt

And still, I sit
A hollow cathedral of longing
Where even enzymes
Whisper 'hunger'
Like forgotten hymns
Not my stomach but our stomachs in a watermelon

My mother boils stones for her children so they sleep
To the promise of bread
Within tomorrow's wind
Two mothers squatting in front of a tent
One says: "I boil stones for my family"
The other says the same
And from the two, "I" grows to "we" in watermelon
Not my mother but my mothers in a watermelon

Sometimes,
I tie rocks to my stomach
Just to fool hunger – soothe its growl
Like mothers hush a crying child
Rocks are our bread
Silence is our meal

At night, men squat by their tents while women and children listen –
    in front of the firewood.
A voice says: *"I have little food"*, another says: *"I have none."*
It can be summed up as one saying: *"We have little food."*
    The other says: *"We have enough to survive."*
Realize that brotherhood of bread connects us.
    That hunger teaches us to say "we" for we are one!

Here,
Bread is life
But life is forbidden
The rusty lock seals the ovens
Blocks the wheat
Blinds the Sky
Even the sun looks down and turns away

Still,
The world speaks in silence,
Their voices clouds that never rain
They deliver statements – not food

No Stars in My Sky

Lina Khattab

There are no stars in my sky
No calm in the waves of my shores
No gentle wind, no warming sun
I am fire – a burning ember
So beware, and be patient
Until you see how the jasmine, stained with my blood
Becomes an olive tree bearing my identity

Be patient
To witness how I am born after a thousand nights and deaths,
To finish a story that will never end

Death tries again and again to rewrite it,
Wants me hungry, afraid, fleeing, alone
Wants to steal my name, my identity
And crush my hope beneath its boots

But how laughable it is −
Does death think I can die,
While my pain still burns
And I've yet to avenge every murdered child,
Every home reduced to dust,
But not yet set alight by my blazing rage?

Death fears me, though I do not fear it −
Even with its gun pointed at my heart.
It fears me because I am truth −
A truth no death can erase.
A truth that flows from my blood into existence,
Passed along by lilies and migrating birds,
Carried by the wind that chants my name.

It fears me because this land loves me, remembers me.
It fears me because it does not love this land like I do,
It never learned how life's narrowness here
Could feel vast.

It never learned how I walk through death and live,
How I raise my flag over the ruins of my home,
How I continue my poem.

I am alive − here −
On a land that knows me,
That I know.
I comfort her, protect her, rebuild her.

I rewrite my melodies
And write of a beautiful hope,
And a dawn that nears.

But still, my tears betray me.
I am not okay.
My country wounds me.
The horizon closes in.

And once again I return,
My embers burning hotter.

Who will put out the fire in my chest?
Who will return the memories and the companions?

I cry — and still, I know I have won,
Even in my loss.
Death has not stolen my voice,
Hunger has not broken my will,
Fear has not made me forget who I am.

I have never forgotten my demands.
I bet my blood,
And on the wall behind which death hides, I write:

I do not forget.

I laugh —
At how the gun turned a dwarf into a giant,
At how humanity has become a tattered rag,
Soft chains.

I am not afraid.
I have stood here many times.
I know injustice so well, it feels familiar.

But still —
I dream of the day
My shores fall calm,
And I put an end to death's story
Once it realizes
I do not die.

That my voice will invade the clouds,
And scatter the hidden rain,
Until existence itself sings with me —
On the path of my return
To a homeland
without death.

We died... you scrolled

Wissam Yousef

Someone asked me, why do you speak out? Why do you write?

Because they want us to die in silence — to vanish without a trace,
    without a story.
We write because writing is resistance.
We share because silence is complicity. Silence is a witness that lies.

Yes, many know there's famine in Gaza —
but knowing isn't enough.
We don't write just so the world "knows".
We write so no one can claim they didn't.
We write so they can't look away without guilt.

We write to expose.
We write to disturb their comfort — to rattle sleeping consciences.
We write so that the child who died of hunger is not forgotten.
So that the hungry have names.
So that the killers are named too.

Cheaper Than Bread

Jood Sabea

Give me bread
a loaf
or even a broken crumb
to live through my hollow days
Give me news
that breathes hope back into my bones
Lie to me
Please
tell me flour is on its way
the war is ending
and place your hand upon my shoulder

whisper softly in my ear,
this time will pass,it will pass
Give me sleep
deep and dreamless
cut me from this life like thread from needle
Wake me
when children no longer cry from hunger
when grown men no longer fall from sorrow
Wake me
when the hungry are fed
when pain is gone
when hope no longer hurts to hold
Give me a thread to dream upon
show me the way
Guide me
is it a sin to dream of flour?
has flour become a prayer?
a wish we whisper in the dark
has my blood turned water in your hands?
My blood
a river now
drowning all it touches
and still you did not stop
My dream became a broken crumb
and you broke it
you broke me
I wander
searching for myself
for my dignity
for a crumb to hush this hunger
for a loaf to bring a child's smile back
I search for a spot of light
to crack this suffocating dark
I search for a past
where children were fed
and fathers stood tall
proud unbowed
Where the city was still a city
and people were still people

not shattered by hunger
I search for a past
where a human life
was never cheaper
than a piece of bread

All I Ask Is to Join the Race

Saad Aldin Ahmed Muhnna

As an engineering student living in Gaza, I no longer feel like myself.
I no longer feel I have worth.
Who thinks about science when there's barely food to eat?
And if there is, it comes at an astronomical price.
Who seeks knowledge when the basics of life are stripped away?
Even my own family has started to see me as a burden,
    an unproductive soul with nothing to offer.
But I am not that.
I'm just someone who dares to dream.

I dream of learning.
I dream of making a difference.
I dream of having a place in this world — nothing more.

I feel like a race car forced to work as a taxi — the engine roars inside,
    but has no choice.
I know I'm not a top student, not exceptional.
But I have the will, the plans, the potential to create something real…
Yet I am shackled.

I'm not asking to win.
All I want…
is the right to fail, to try, to fall, and rise again.
I want to learn — even if it's just a little, every day.
Even one step forward, however small.

I don't ask for medals.
Just…
Let me join the race.

Bread of Dreams in the Blaze of Darkness

Rawan Marwan Omar Matar

In Gaza, we were children of dignity and pride,
Our homes were warm, and laughter lived inside.
Our streets were alive, our hearts kind and bright,
We lived with humble longing, generous in light.

But the skies suddenly flamed with fire,
And everything changed – deprivation grew dire.
The occupation came like a savage storm,
Shattering our childhood in a ruthless form.

Yet what wounds me most, beyond the despair,
Is hunger – that daylight killer laid bare.
A slow, merciless siege, so cruel, so grim,
Extinguishing spirits, leaving lives dim.

First, the meat vanished – then fruit was no more,
Even bread became a silent wish at our core.
Not even the wealthy can find food to eat,
Money frozen, minds blind in deceit.

We now fight for a single bite of bread,
Killed as we battle hunger with heads held.
They allow in a truck of flour or two,
Then bomb us as we rush with longing anew.

They call it aid… as we are slaughtered instead,
We know these are massacres – our tears have bled.
We line up with fragile threads of hope,
Only to fall – one martyr after another elopes.

A child starved to death in silence so cruel,
A mother miscarried – her ribs a trembling tool.
An elder fainted, the youth collapsed,
Our tears-soaked streets, as hearts unclasped.

I eat less so my siblings can be fed,
I watch my mother starve in silence widespread.
My father wrestles for our daily bread,
While silent agony tears through what's unsaid.

This is not poverty – it's a siege,
Not helplessness – but betrayal and fatigue.
Where are you, O nation of a billion souls?
Would a starving bird go unseen in your roles?

May God bless Omar, the just and grand,
Who starved so every child might understand.
But today, hearts are hardened like stone,
And the doors of mercy remain unknown.

We can no longer endure this pain,
Our cursed reality defies even the pen's refrain.
But still we remain – through all the despair -
Clutching hope, and shouting into the voided air.

Our Day

Ahmed Raed Mohammed Farhan

Day after a day, we are sacrificed,
Day after a day, we lost a light from our eyes,
Day after a day, The hope stop fly
Day after a day close from our us the die
And we are keeping ask one question, who will stop the genocide

If you want flour come forward

Wissam Yousef

It wasn't fiction.
It wasn't a movie.
It was Gaza – bleeding, starving, betrayed.

On a suffocating, gray afternoon, young men emerged from the ashes
of war, from tents torn by wind and fire in northern Gaza. Barefoot,
hollow-eyed, they ran not for escape – but for survival.

They were told: "There is flour at Al-Waha."
And in Gaza, flour is life.

Witnesses say they approached the aid point — carrying no weapons,
only the weight of hunger and the last flickers of hope.

Then a voice echoed from afar:
"Raise your hands… walk past the tanks…
If you want flour, come forward."

Around 200 souls moved toward that promise — a promise wrapped
in steel and deception. Step by step, like a procession of ghosts,
they advanced. And just as their fingers brushed the sacks of flour —
bullets tore through the air.

In mere seconds, the ground was soaked with blood.
Over 40 were slaughtered, their dreams shattered in silence.
More than 100 wounded, crawling for breath beneath smoke
        and screams.

No warning. No mercy. No humanity.
Just a trap — where hunger was the bait and death was the reward.

This was not a scene from distant history.
This is Gaza — now.
Where a sack of flour costs your life,
Where starvation is weaponized,
Where human beings are hunted for daring to want bread.

This is not a tragedy.
This is a crime against humanity.
And the world watched.
And the world stayed silent.

▲ Mariam Marwan Malaka

Lost Wish

Mariam Marwan Malaka

And I wished I had gone before you – or with you.
I wished I had kissed the brow of freedom.
I wished my kiss had come in your presence.
I wished, when sleep slips past grief-heavy lids, it would find you
waiting.
I wished there had been, at the very least, a farewell -
One in which I could weep myself to death,
So they might carry my coffin and yours, side by side.

It was a cruel departure, beloved -
One whose cruelty clings to every tick of the clock -
Relentless, unyielding.

What kind of departure was this?
On the banks of farewell and departure both,
Thin hands hung suspended,
Scalding tears were crucified,
And the souls of the lovers crumbled.

O gentle one, O blessed one…
You were once a dream -
And in recent days, a nightmare that would not pass.

The soul fails to make sense of it.
A question wrapped in a thousand fears
Leaves you fragmented -
Torn from yourself.

Where did you go without me?
What about me?
How long must I keep asking?

The moan of memory rises with every dawn.
I freeze in place,
And waste away,
Feeble – so feeble.

I tend to wounds I never caused.
All I ever did was walk into life alone…
And so I became one with the darkness.

What now?

In your leaving, did you find eternal bliss?
In your leaving, did you find a faithful lover?
In your leaving, did you leave behind a place
For the beloved once bound by fleeting love
And the eternal ache of parting?

Memories linger within her,
Tormented by a yearning chained in naked longing.
A dream wraps itself around her on the edge of delusion -
Dancing for moments, collapsing the next.

What reason is there in such love?

A beloved in a mirage…
And a lover lost to eternity.

When words fail

Mariam Marwan Malaka

I no longer believe in words,
And there is no way to steady the letters here.
I've grown used only to the grey in life -
For feeling has truly faded,
And pleasures flutter past me like ash in the wind.

O defier of tears,
Lend me a portion of your defiance -
Just the excess, the part you no longer need.

Pain intensifies,
The soul retreats,
And the eyes take their due in floods of tears.
But embraces -
They do not return.
They resume only after life has passed.

O human,
Be a dreamer,
So that you may earn the embraces you deserve -
At the hour of death.

Who said death is to be feared?

Let me speak of my death,
O you who still live, in body and in heart.

When I die,
I will meet the beloved,
And longing shall finally surrender to the one it chased.

Yes -
I will meet the beloved,
And bury my face in his vast chest.
I will say:
"I have come to you, my love.
I have come -
Long have the ages worn me thin, ground me down."

You will tell me how long you waited,
And I will tell you of the tears that humbled me.

I will tell you of the nights when the clock struck remembrance,
When the breeze of happy moments returned,
And storms of your smile swept through my thoughts.

I will tell you of tears falling endlessly,
Until my eyelids wilted into sleep -
Wishing never to wake again,
As dreams dissolved in the Kabul of time.

I will tell you of the hours of longing,
And the claws of yearning.

I will tell you of sleeping beside your grave -
A temporary death,
Hoping you might come back to me.

I shake the sands of your grave and cry:
"Come back! I miss you... I am alone."

I will tell you of the wish to die a thousand times -
To die torn into pieces,
Rather than live aching for a beloved
Who now rests content with his Lord.

I will tell you,
And tell you still -
The tale stretches on.

And the tale stretches on...
While the heart pleads:

I no longer believe in words,
And there is no way to steady the letters.

In Mourning

Mariam Marwan Malaka

As I still lie in bed,
Recovering from the wound left by a blow to the soul,
Here – blood mingles with tears,
And farewell kisses I was denied
Are trapped between the lines, where letters refuse to flow.
So I write nothing.
For you – you – are no longer here.

My pen wails in grief, mourning you:
"Why do you write?
Is he still reading?
If he no longer reads,
Then lay me aside and let weeping be your only language."

Alone -
And I shall remain alone.

I gaze into the sky
And see our reflection held in a cloud -
A cloud that refused to stay.

It speaks to me of parting, and of love for martyrdom.
I reply,
"I fear separation – I've never known it!"
And you answer,
"Through me, you shall know it now."

And here I am -
Torn apart in its sea,
Unable to catch my breath,
Unable to hear even an echo.

Against my will, I write now -
Spilling out the stuffing of sorrowful words.
One moment, my pen rebels,
Mounts its steed and flees – leaving not a single letter behind.
Another moment, it sneaks a verse about you –
And the languages rage in protest.

In mourning you -
Everyone writes,
While I clutch my hands tightly,
Trying not to write.

In mourning you -
Everyone weeps,
While I remain frozen in the moment your presence became a memory.

I press your words to my chest -
Words that left with you,
Along with promises, dreams, and light.

Still, I feel you beside me -
Mending my wounds,
Easing my sighs and moans.

I have not accepted your departure yet -
How could I?
When all that is called acceptance feels like defiance!

Silent Graves

Mariam Marwan Malaka

Where pallor dwells, and graves abide -
The gravekeeper gazes with indifference.
The pavement is stained in blood -
I walk slowly, my steps slipping away.
A fountain of blood…
Unreckoned, uncontained.

The beginning ends
With a quiet, overwhelming weeping.
Beside the dead, I lie.
The moon is luminous -
But I miss *your* light in it.

I try to avoid the stench of the dead -
But what's the use?

What I wouldn't give
For life to return for just a moment -
A moment to embrace flesh, not earth.

The soul is soul -
And its torment, merciless.

I have brought you fresh flowers.
Come back to life!
Madness has seized the mind.

Even the graves grow weary of those of us who linger -
They grow tired of our cries.
This is no longer a place to sleep.

The soul's unrest has drifted
Over a withered heart.
The darkness of your absence
Has crushed my right to live.

Loss is bitter – so bitter.
Yet even bitterness dissolves
In the intoxication of fleeting moments.

From the old, death-haunted house, I mourn -
Threads of desolation hang in every corner.
The corpses of century-old spiders multiply,
And the cry of the owl draws near.

Inevitably, the scorpions sail,
And soon -
Time will drown.

All my torments,
All the crossings of swords -
They mean nothing
Compared to the memory
Of one single moment you spent with me.

Since you left -
I have not existed.

Or perhaps the beginning

Mariam Marwan Malaka

The war will end...
The temporary sorrow will fade...
And that eternal emptiness will settle into place.

But I -
I will remain, waiting for the trace of your tender spirit
    beside my heart,
Sifting now and then through memories that refuse to carry on.

It will end...
And I will remain -
The only one lingering by your grave,
Bringing fresh flowers and whispering:

Take me with you – to you – into the shelter of your ribs, like always.
You draw from me every sigh and sob,
And you make room for them.

It will end...
And I will still dwell in the corners of death,
Like one yearning for your return.
As for the corners of love -
I am a vagabond, a vagabond, a vagabond...
Misled along the path,
Blind in heart, and sight soon follows.

A person is humiliated in proportion to their longing -
And I, by mine, am annihilated.

Where are you?
Who will carry this shackled misery from me?
Each night I exhale from the brutality of feeling -
And it breaks me.
How long will you remain there – while I remain here?

Will this false distance ever vanish?

I am a prisoner of a frail life -
A life without you, without your love.
Nothing remains but drought.

I am the falling one – the lover -
Found by love in the depths of the soul,
Saying to me:

"Feel the stings of parting."

But what am I to do?
For what sin am I crushed?
How is it that such things are done to me,
When they are done to no one else?

It will end.

Gaza...When She Was Enough To Make Us Happy

Aseel Shaban Nahed Elmabhouh

Gaza? She was the whole world.

I used to wake up to the voices of street vendors in the alley,
To the scent of my mother's bread,
And to my brother's laughter as he plotted how we'd sneak off
    to the sea before the sun woke up.

Gaza was simple, warm, honest.
We never asked much of her -
Because she gave us everything:
The love of people,
The warmth of our homes,
The light of candles even when the power was out,
As if to tell us, "Don't be afraid, the light is still inside you."

Gaza meant safety – despite the poverty.
Joy – despite the exhaustion.
Hope – despite everything.
She was enough for us.

The sea was an embrace.
The sky wasn't frightening.
And laughter – laughter was real.

Everything in her was kind...
The people, the streets, even the crowds,
Even the stones we sat on at the edge of the house.

But suddenly -
It was as if we'd woken up from a dream.

The homes that once meant safety... collapsed.
The faces we knew... disappeared.
The streets we used to race through... turned into rivers of blood.

Gaza today is not the Gaza we knew.
She's become a wound in the heart,
A shattered image.
Everything feels heavy now...
Even the air.
Even sleep.
Even hope.

The people have changed -
Or maybe they've just grown tired.
The children don't play like they used to -
They know far more than their age should allow.
And the sounds we once loved
Have turned into explosions,
Screams,
And breaking news alerts.

And when I asked myself,
"Why? What happened? Who's to blame?"
I couldn't find a single answer.

Every side pulled Gaza toward itself.
Every party decided our fate – without asking us.
And everyone justified their pain... with our blood.

Those with weapons – used them.
Those with power – ignored us.
And those who promised us life – handed us over to death.

And we?
We got lost in between.

I don't want to accuse,
I don't want to name names,
But I *do* know that everyone was wrong.
Wrong to belittle our lives,
Wrong to exploit us,
Wrong to forget us,
Wrong to make us bear the cost – alone.

Gaza is not just breaking news.
Not just a besieged strip of land.
Gaza was the dream that was enough for us -
But today, even dreaming has become forbidden.

Before the war,
I was studying at one of the most beautiful universities.
I had ambition, plans, a future I was building step by step,
With every book,
Every lecture.

But everything stopped.
My studies stopped -
Just like my life.

And yet… I didn't give up.
I still dream of finishing my university education abroad -
Far from fear,
Far from the noise.

I want to study English translation,
The major I love -
Because I believe words have power.
And I want to use mine to carry my voice,
To carry our story to the world.

I'm just one voice from Gaza -
But maybe…
Maybe someone will hear me.
Someone will believe in the dream,
Will feel the loss,
And will see in me a spark of hope rising from beneath the rubble.

If I shall be a number

Dania Abusaqer

If I shall be a number,
can you tell me what number?
Am I one digit?
Two, three, four, five, six, or seven digits?
Can you tell me when it's my turn?
If it's today, shall I say goodbye to yesterday?
Throw all dreams away,
leave old pictures in the past,
eat more – no fear of gaining weight,
or breaking the scale with the softness I've grown into,
widen my heart and spread love,
smile at strangers without reason,
forgive everyone who left without goodbye,
hug longer, let time stretch in my arms,
dance with no music,
let silence sing for me,
burn every "what if" in a quiet ceremony,
make peace with the mirror,
whisper thank you to God,
pray for the last time,
and maybe, just maybe,
plant a seed where I thought nothing would grow.
And write my last poem – to be remembered.

Between Hunger and Silence

Samah Mustafa Yousef Bashir

Not from the burden of years,
But from bellies collapsing into their own emptiness -
As if they were devouring air.

The children stopped playing,

Not because they were tired,
But because laughter, too,
Requires calories.

They shut down the swings in the alley -
Joy has become a luxury.
Even the sound of a football
Is annoying now
To someone who hasn't eaten in two days.

And the vendors?
There they are – polishing their tongues
With promises,
Raising the price of bread
Each time a soul falls.
They smile as they tally the hungry's account,
As if hunger were a business,
And the people – just a banquet.

As for the occupation,
And those who dare speak in our name…
They are the lords of the stage -
Directing scenes of negotiation,
With the makeup of a ceasefire,
And the script of aid on the way.
They give us a dose of anesthetic at every meeting,
So we stay half-conscious,
Half-dead,
Half-hopeful.

They tell us:
"Calm in exchange for bread."
And so we hand them our silence -
And with it, they take the last of our crumbs.

They say:
"Patience is the key to relief."
So we wait – longer,
Until the key explodes inside the lock.

They say:
"The truce is near."

And we believe them.
We ready our stomachs
For a meal postponed…
We wait…
And hunger grows,
While words shrink.

In Gaza,
Hunger does not breed submission.
It awakens the revolution from its sleep.
We will not die of hunger -
We will live as fire.

And when the world has had its fill of denying us,
We will be -
The new wheat,
And the flame that cooks
The feast to come.

Epilogue

In the heart of suffering, words are born – and from beneath the rubble, creativity rises.

This book is more than a collection of written pages; it is the echo of resilient souls and the cries of pens that spoke when voices were silenced.

Amidst Gaza's devastation, a group of our students put pen to paper, capturing the raw truth of life under siege. Their words reflect the unbearable suffering they endure – not only as students striving for knowledge, but as native residents trapped in a relentless war of starvation and erasure. This book is a mirror to their pain, a testimony to their resilience, and a plea for the world to listen.

Professor Dr. Omar Kh. Melad
President of Al-Azhar University – Gaza
2 August 2025

Acknowledgement

We dedicate this book to all the students who contributed to it, and to those who could not contribute to it because their lives were tragically cut short, along with their university staff members and families.

We are especially grateful to Mona J. Al Khazendar from Al Azhar University, Gaza for her vital support in gathering these writings from students in Gaza – an effort of profound value and dedication.

Our heartfelt thanks also go to the remarkable individuals whose linguistic expertise, cultural sensitivity, and generous care made the proofreading and translation of these texts possible.

To Samira Bouyagoub, Ielyaa Elshahri, Nisreen Elshahri, Alya Barghathi, and Dalia Taleb – thank you for your commitment to preserving the emotional depth, nuance, and authenticity of every voice shared here. As fluent speakers of Arabic and English with deep insight into language and meaning, your contribution ensured that these stories reached the world with honesty, clarity, and dignity.

And finally, to Nicky Robertson – my heartfelt thanks for your unwavering encouragement and steadfast support in bringing this book to life.

This book carries many hearts. Thank you for helping us carry them with care.

By God, a heart is terrified by separation, sorrowful, and an eyelid soaked with tears.

– Mariam Marwan Malaka

EU Safety Information

Publisher: Daraja Press, PO BOX 99900 BM 735 664 Wakefield, QC J0X 0C2, Canada

info@darajapress.com | https://darajapress.com

EU Authorized GPSR Representative: Easy Access System Europe - Mustamäe tee 50, 10621 Tallinn, Estonia, gpsr.requests@easprojec:.com

For EU product safety concerns, please contact us at info@darajapress.com

Printed and bound in the United Kingdom

02/10/2025

01967400-0001